the PROSPEROUS LEADER

the
PROSPEROUS
LEADER

How Smart People Achieve Success

JACOB M. ENGEL
with Jeffrey A. Krames

NEW YORK

the PROSPEROUS LEADER
How Smart People Achieve Success

© 2015 Jacob M. Engel.

Published in New York, New York, by Morgan James Publishing. Morgan James and The Entrepreneurial Publisher are trademarks of Morgan James, LLC.
www.MorganJamesPublishing.com

The Morgan James Speakers Group can bring authors to your live event. For more information or to book an event visit The Morgan James Speakers Group at www.TheMorganJamesSpeakersGroup.com.

A FREE eBook edition is available
with the purchase of this print book

CLEARLY PRINT YOUR NAME IN THE BOX ABOVE

Instructions to claim your free eBook edition:
1. Download the BitLit app for Android or iOS
2. Write your name in UPPER CASE in the box
3. Use the BitLit app to submit a photo
4. Download your eBook to any device

ISBN 978-1-63047-273-3 paperback
ISBN 978-1-63047-274-0 eBook
ISBN 978-1-63047-275-7 hardcover
Library of Congress Control Number:
2014940588

Cover Design by:
Rachel Lopez
www.r2cdesign.com

Interior Design by:
Bonnie Bushman
bonnie@caboodlegraphics.com

In an effort to support local communities, raise awareness and funds, Morgan James Publishing donates a percentage of all book sales for the life of each book to Habitat for Humanity Peninsula and Greater Williamsburg.

Get involved today, visit
www.MorganJamesBuilds.com

Habitat
for Humanity®
Peninsula and
Greater Williamsburg
Building Partner

CONTENTS

FOREWORD

Prosperity is an interesting topic to address today, especially with so many people focused on survival, with so much talk about scarcity, and with the reality that our future depends on our unique individual abilities. Jacob Engel provides us with an important look at the skills necessary—and how to acquire them—to create our own prosperity while staying true to our responsibilities as managers and leaders.

In practice I have found that people and organizations create their own destiny based on their style and focus. Simply put, people and organizations fail, they succeed, or in rare (too rare) situations, they are able to prosper. In this book Jacob takes the time necessary to assist you in your journey toward achieving prosperity.

To fully appreciate prosperity, it's important to have a clear definition of *prosperity*. As defined by Merriam-Webster's Collegiate Dictionary, it is the state of being successful or thriving. Prosperity often encompasses wealth but also includes other factors to varying degrees, such as happiness and health. As we better understand what prosperity means, we can appreciate what it takes to achieve prosperity in our lives and our businesses.

How then do we avoid the failure that many have experienced?

How do we achieve success as some have?

How do we aspire to and then achieve the prosperity few do?

As you read Jacob Engel's book, you will come across a variety of models and have numerous "aha" moments. The models will prove useful as they provide the structure, organization, and ability to achieve prosperity with new insights and skills. The aha moments will help to crystallize your thoughts into understandable, bite-size pieces. It's that moment when the light bulb goes on and you finally see what had been there all along, but you now understand. Just as when the blurry becomes the clear in an eye exam, you will have a new vision to move toward.

Failure, success, and prosperity as outcomes can come from a business model that I developed through my work with entrepreneurs and their organizations (See chapter 13).

The Six Cs of communication in organizational growth and development show a clear correlation between the style of the entrepreneur and whether or not prosperity can be realistically achieved.

Basically, organizations that have internal conflict and competition will fail. Those that can attain internal compliance and communication succeed. And those that internally cooperate and collaborate will prosper.

COMMUNICATION
The Six Cs

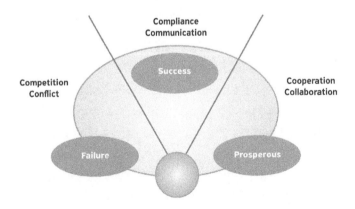

Prosperity is achievable if we are willing to accept accountability and are able to learn new skills. Jacob Engel has done an outstanding service by providing this book to each of us. Please read it, adapt its principles to your situation, and *prosper*.

—**Roy Cammarano**, Author of *Entrepreneurial Transitions: From Entrepreneurial Genius to Visionary Leadership*

ACKNOWLEDGMENTS

As a religious person, I am indebted to my creator, without whom nothing is possible and with whom everything is possible.

I owe a great debt to my parents. My father, who was a Holocaust survivor and came to this country without family, language, or money created his own prosperity. (See profiles of a role model). He went on to build a huge enterprise with his surviving family and empowered others to do the same. But he died in his prime, at age sixty-five. My mother is still my biggest fan. In our daily phone calls, she wants to know if I'm "teaching today." She avidly reads my articles and wants to know when my book is being published. So here it is.

I want to thank Ruth Lichtenstein, Rachel Roth, and their great staff for giving me the opportunity to publish my articles in their *Hamodia* weekly newspaper and the excellent feedback I got from their readership worldwide.

I thank my partners (M. K. and D. G.) for supporting this initiative and Robert Kaplan, Shayna Horowitz, and Jenny Astwood (graphics) for developing and creating the "Create Prosperity" idea, logo, and tagline.

Special thanks to Michael Schmutter and my assistant M. Smith for their great assistance in helping write and editing these articles.

In closing, I would like to mention my gratitude to my mentor and coach, Roy Cammarano, who has written a beautiful foreword, but more importantly has given me the courage and encouragement to write this book. Thanks, Roy.

In my search for a business author who could help evaluate what parts of the book needed reworking and what was missing, I came across a greatly inspiring and world-renowned author, Jeffrey Krames. Jeffrey and his crew have undertaken to read my manuscript chapter by chapter and have added valuable additions to the book. Jeffrey has been very kind and gracious in allowing me to add his name to the book, for which I thank him.

I want to thank Alan Lovins, PhD for reading and adding valuable insights.

Finding a Publisher is no easy feat for a first time author. In my search I was very fortunate to come across the website of Morgan James Publishing which its founder David Hancock, calls the "Entrepreneurs" publisher. David, Jim Howard (his publisher), and his team of Margo and Bethany, have done an excellent job for which I thank them for!

Lastly and most importantly, I owe a great amount of gratitude to my wife, children, and grandchildren.

And thank you, the reader.

PREFACE

I was recently in West Palm Beach, and while standing in line at a health spa, I saw someone in front of me with a nametag that read, "Michael Gerber".

He looked very approachable, so I asked him, "Are you *THE* Michael Gerber?"

He said *yes*.

"Of *The E-Myth* fame?" I asked.

He answered, "Yes," and then he invited me to his table. I was very excited to hear him expound on his vision of creating the Entrepreneur University and his work in training entrepreneurs worldwide, and he invited me to San Marcos, where he runs his seminars.

I then had the *chuptzah* to ask him if he would read my manuscript, and he said, "You know? I get many requests every day and I say *no*, but to you I'll say *yes*!"

I didn't know what I was getting myself into.

"Candidly," he told me after reading it, "I was more interested in your father's story [brought up briefly in the introduction] than I was in yours. This book on leadership could be—should be—your father's story."

I had also asked him to suggest a title. He suggested *"Leadership Lessons from the Holocaust (and How They Apply to the world Today)"*.

"You see," he explained, "the Jews who suffered in Germany, had, in a cruel way, participated in their own demise, by not believing that what was *about* to happen *could* happen. The same thing is true of the people in Detroit (Have you seen the photographs of that horror city?).

"See how easily it can happen?

That's your book. It's about leadership, but leadership in our everyday lives. You must write about leadership not as an *idea*, but as an action that we—each of us—must immediately take. Why is it that we can't see that with over 17 trillion dollars in debt (incurred in just 20 years!) and an accrued un-payable liability of more than 90 trillion dollars, that we, in this country, are going bankrupt—in fact, actually *are* bankrupt?

"Why can't we see it? Because we choose not to. That's one of the most important leadership lessons from the Holocaust: We chose *not* to! And so the indescribable happened!

"Write a *real* book, Jacob!"

So here it is.

Introduction

Profile of a Role Model:
From Holocaust Horrors to
Prosperous Leadership
Barry Engel 1928-1994

My father was a true role model—not only for our family, but also for our community and beyond. He made it out of the horrors of the Holocaust and went on the create and (re) build a legacy that not only was a legend in his lifetime, but that even now, almost 20 years later, still remains! I recently read a great book "Give and Take" by Adam Grant. He divides people into 3 categories: *Givers*, *Takers*, and *Matchers*. In reading his description of a *Giver*, he portrayed my father perfectly!

Unthinkable Tragedy

Barry Engel was born in 1928 in Tokay, Hungary—a pastoral town known for its wonderful vineyards and excellent wine. His boyhood was no different than that of any other boy growing up in Eastern Europe in the late 1920s and early 1930s. His family enjoyed a life of relative wealth and prominence. That is, until Hitler came to power in Germany and conquered country after country, eventually threatening even the world powers. By the time the Allies succeeded in defeating the Nazi regime, 6 million Jews and millions of others had been murdered in the infamous death camps. Barry's own father, Jeno (Jacob) Engel, had been rounded up in Budapest and sent to the Auschwitz Death Camp, from which he never returned.

Rising From the Ashes

After the Allies brought the Third Reich to its knees and liberated the camps, the survivors tried returning to their homes to start new lives. For most of them, this hope could not be realized, as they discovered they were not really welcome in their own countries either.

After attempting to settle in several countries, my father came to New York, with no money, language or family. (His mother and siblings would come later.) Years later, he would jokingly reminisce that even the clothes on his back, which he'd bought right before leaving Hungary, he had to throw out, because it made him look like a "Greenhorn", which was a label that immigrants tried very hard to avoid.

A Dream Comes True

My father was able to find a job on the Lower East Side, working for a spice-importing company called "Schoenfeld & Sons". The owner of the company, Mr. Schoenfeld, encouraged him to go out on his own, so my father opened a spice shop in Brooklyn with his mother and eventually his younger brother. He told Mr. Schoenfeld that one day, he would bring in a million dollars a year in sales.

From the storefront in Brooklyn, his business eventually moved up to a factory and warehouse in Queens, then to a larger factory and warehouse in Brooklyn, and then to an even larger facility in New Jersey, eventually growing to encompass two facilities and many warehouses. The company very quickly surpassed the million-dollar mark and continued to grow many times over. He was able to dream and dream big.

A Community Activist

My father was also very prominent and active in community affairs, and was especially fond of helping others who struggled in their careers or business. He helped many people start and run successful companies, and he always reminisced how fortunate they were, having an uncle in New York loan them three thousand dollars (in *1955* dollars) to help their fledging businesses. His motto became, "If you were blessed, make sure to help others."

A Model of Humility

Though he dealt in millions and gave away millions to charity, he never felt the need to "show off". He lived a simple (albeit comfortable) life, and enjoyed his wealth in a healthy way. He didn't think it was beyond his dignity to fundraise for his favorite charities (which were many), and though he was often the largest donor, he was always ready to help the causes he believed in. His motto was, "Charity is obligatory and helping others was mandatory."

A Pillar of Courage

Though my father was a peaceful man, he never shirked from standing up for what was right, and wouldn't tolerate those who didn't. His motto was, "If you are put in a situation that requires courage, then stand up and be courageous."

Yes, my father had many mottoes. In looking back at his ideas, I've been able trace them back to some of history's greatest philosophers and leaders. But, as he didn't have any formal education (or its contemporary substitute— the internet), these were ideas that he created in his own mind but were still solid principles that helped him shape his own leadership personality:

1. *Never confuse efforts for results!*
2. *Remember and be true to your roots. Understand your core essence and responsibilities.*
3. *Find a balance between others' needs and your own.*
4. *There are two secrets to success: Having great ambitions and having an even greater discipline to <u>achieve</u> those ambitions.*
5. *Be humble. If you were given gifts, use them to <u>help</u> others, not to <u>spite</u> others.*
6. *Have an open mind to learn new things. If all you do is talk, you are just repeating what you know. If you listen, you learn new things.*
7. *Anyone (idiot) can sell a dollar for ninety-nine cents.*
8. *Know what you stand for and what you <u>won't</u> stand for. If you're in a leadership position, think of the impact of doing the right thing.*
9. *Think past your nose. Have a wider vision, and don't think small.*
10. *Always give back to the community. Everyone needs someone to help him at one time or another.*

Years ago, when I first became interested in the subject of leadership, I came across the bestselling book *The 7 Habits of Highly Effective People* by Stephen R. Covey. In his book, he talks about how he immersed himself in a study of success literature of the past 200 years and noticed a pattern in the content: Almost all the literature focused on what Covey calls "character ethic" attributes—humility, integrity, courage, patience, compassion, and the Golden Rule ("Do unto others…").

"These basic principles of effective living and true success depended on integrating these principles into one's character," Covey says.

In his last book, The 3rd Alternative, he gives his own definition of prosperity, which is the essence of this book:

Money is only one kind of wealth, a mark of secondary success. Primary success, as I've said before, arises from our character, and is measured in terms of the contributions we make. Integrity, honesty, hard work, and compassion for others—if we live by these principles, we will never be poor in primary. In a world of such people, no one would be poor, not even the weak and disabled. This kind of wealth is primary wealth. Often (there's no guarantee) secondary wealth follows as a natural consequence. The assets that lead to material prosperity have never changed; they are character, education, skills and relationships developed over time, and patience.

There are natural laws at work here, and those that live by them can be both humble and confident at the same time. It's true that some people get rich without these assets, through birth, luck, or conniving and it's easy to get bitter over it. But if I see myself as a victim, [then] I will wait for society to become "fair" rather than developing those primary assets that lead to prosperity (p. 355).

What wisdom!

This book came about after I had taken early retirement as the COO of a large food and real estate family-owned enterprise. The recent economic downturn had hit hard; there were mass layoffs, and many people were desperate for work. I joined a community-based initiative that helped the recently unemployed find jobs. While my efforts were rewarding, I found myself thinking, "What can we do that will both enhance their marketable skills and allow them to go on to do better and greater things?"

In addition, many were interested in becoming their own bosses so they would not be as susceptible to mass layoffs. Entrepreneurship is becoming more and more important in the new economy. On top of that, as the landscape of business has changed, we exist now in what's called a "flat world". In order to succeed, it's not enough to just have a cool idea. Entrepreneurs need to know how to build—and more importantly, how to *lead*. Leadership and management skills are more essential than ever, but unfortunately, they are not taught in schools. Additionally, leadership skills are very much in demand in startups, and even more so in growing businesses. In fact, most business owners I speak to complain that they have a very hard time finding good employees that take initiative and responsibility. (In today's world, everyone is their own CEO.)

This is what we aimed to teach. We started a pilot program of fifteen adults who ranged from their early twenties to late forties. Those who could not afford to pay received a scholarship, which we funded. Those that could afford to pay paid only the direct costs; we funded the rest. In the six months that this intensive effort went on, we brought in a slew of world-renowned trainers from various well-known talent-development organizations. The participants were reinvigorated, as now they had marketable skills, especially in management and leadership.

Many of them found jobs right away. One participant told me, "I would never have had the courage and self-confidence to interview for a management position. Now I've found my dream job."

The participants showed up for all of the trainings and seminars. They were invigorated by the new learning experience, and we were excited about our "teaching them how to fish." One participant, David Hess, told me that while he was very interested in becoming his own boss, he didn't have the type of training needed to start and run his own company. It was only after the six months of training and mentorship that he was able to start his own business.

The challenge was that outside trainers are expensive for someone who is out of a job, and the logistics of flying trainers in is tough and costly. This inspired me to start my own training organization. In the years since, our organization has trained many hundreds of participants.

In addition, over time, we realized that business owners need one-on-one mentoring to help them implement what they have learned, as the theories in our basic training help them understand what needs to be done, but as my father said, actually getting it done is a huge challenge. So we now include business consulting and coaching as well.

Purpose of this book.

The purpose of this book is to share my experience and the lessons I learned from my father, both in running a large, high-growth, family-owned enterprise, and in helping others run successful organizations. While many of the lessons shared here (some of which I quote directly) are available elsewhere, I also try to distill and simplify the many complex and sometimes hard-to-understand theories, as well as tell the stories of our own participants' success. What I've found is that most people struggle with taking the many (and sometimes *too* many) good ideas and implementing them into their own organizations. It takes a combination of actually having run businesses and having implemented these theories to see what works and what doesn't, as not all tools can be used for every situation. I hope that my book will help inspire and guide you to make it happen.

Why do Leaders and Managers struggle?

Leaders and managers struggle because many have never been trained or coached in what management or leadership is all about. I particularly like what Peter Drucker said: "Leadership is doing the right things; management is doing things right." Or, as Covey put it, "*Effectiveness* is doing the right thing; *efficiency* is doing things right."

Why are goals important?

Those who don't have a goal for their life, career, and so on, end up in the same place over and over. There's a quote that is attributed to Einstein: "*Insanity* is doing the same things over and over and expecting different results." We must help our children, students, and employees define their goals and help them detect their mission in life. If our homes and our schools aren't helping our children figure out their goals, it's no wonder that they end up disenchanted, disconnected, and searching for meaning (usually after a layoff or during a midlife crisis).

The Talmud—the central text of Rabbinic Judaism—includes this intriguing passage:

I was traveling, and I met a child at a crossroads. I asked him, "Which way to the city?" and he answered, "This way is short and long, and that way is long and short." I took the "short and long" way. I soon neared the city but found my approach obstructed by gardens and orchards. So I retraced my steps and said to the child, "My son, did you not tell me that this is the short way?" Answered the child, "Did I not tell you that it is also long?"

The Book of Proverbs has a similar quote that says: "[People] travel paths that go nowhere, wandering in a maze of detours and dead ends."

I've developed a small drawing (see below) that I use to illustrate what happens when people just try to find the easiest solution, or "path of least resistance", instead of first defining their goals, purpose, or mission, and then figuring out a clear path and a time frame to achieve it.

Why do we fail?

People tend to be interested in learning shortcuts, also known as the "quick and dirty" or the "tricks of the trade", but they don't learn the trade itself. Too many believe that the only way to make money is by being conniving, dishonest, or unethical. The news continuously heralds the sins and embarrassments of our various religious, political, and business leaders, but rarely touts their honesty and integrity. Those traits certainly never make it to the front pages, and rarely, if ever, to the back pages.

As Edmund Burke said, "All that is required for evil to prevail is for good men to do nothing."

My mission is to change the perception that good people have no voice and therefore, do nothing. In this book, I describe the journey of many aspiring *Prosperous* leaders who have made the decision to *create their own prosperity.* They have learned how to understand their strengths and abilities and how to help others do the same. They have developed their character as the ethical base of a leader by living with integrity and adhering to a set of principles. They have taken seminars, and they have read books to further their education. They have looked honestly at their skills and at the market to determine what they should relearn and what new material they need to learn. They have invested in true and open relationships over time. They have endured with patience, as even overnight success is never overnight. They have realized that desperate people do desperate things and that learning only the "tricks of the trade" can lead to dishonest or disingenuous behavior. They all achieved *primary wealth*, as Covey defined it, many also achieved secondary wealth, and some have achieved *great* wealth.

How?

"How?" you may ask. By creating true value for their clients, by treating all people—especially employees—with respect, by being open and honest in all communications, by having integrity and a sense of purpose, and by having the staying power and conviction to make all of this the foundation on which they have been able to build huge enterprises that have endured over time (*see Chapter 20*). These people are the ones that drive our economy forward, tend to be the most charitable, and create prosperity for their organizations, communities, and our countries.

This book is about them and their journey. If you're about to begin, are in the process, or are at the end, you will identify with the stories and eventually create your own sense of prosperous leadership.

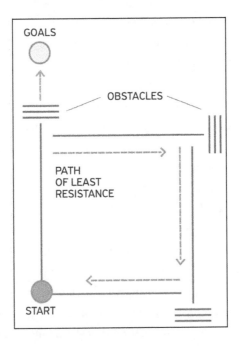

GOALS

OBSTACLES

PATH
OF LEAST
RESISTANCE

START

PART 1

FINDING YOUR STRENGTHS
(And Weaknesses)

Chapter 1

KNOW YOURSELF
TO LEAD OTHERS

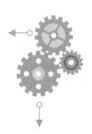

"Know thyself"
—Benjamin Franklin

Know thyself" is a well-known motto attributed to Benjamin
Franklin, and it serves as an essential basis for growth.
Understanding yourself and those around you will help you
effectively manage your employees, which will ultimately help you grow
your business.

Organizations, regardless of their level of success, depend on the founders
or owners to be very honest to themselves about their strengths and weaknesses.
There is a saying "that children and employees know a lot more about their
parents and bosses, then they know about their children and employees." We
all have our strengths and weaknesses and the most successful people are those
that build on their strengths and mitigate their weaknesses.

Peter Drucker in *The Effective Executive* says "The effective executive
makes strength productive. He knows that one cannot build on weakness.

To achieve results, one has to use all of the available strengths—the strengths of associates, the strengths of the superior, and one's own strengths. These strengths are the true opportunities. To make strength productive is the unique purpose of organization. It cannot, of course, overcome the weaknesses with which each of us is abundantly endowed. But it can make them irrelevant. Its task is to use the strength of each man as a building block for joint performance" (See chapter 4).

I once read a great book by Dr. Miriam Adahan called *Living with Difficult People—Including Yourself.* The implication of the title is correct; in many cases we see ourselves doing everything right, and it's the *other* person that needs to change. That's how *the other person* sees it too. Getting to know yourself requires serious thought and effective tools.

One of the most widely used evaluations is aptitude testing. *Aptitude* refers to our innate personality, which usually doesn't change much over our lifetime. We all have behaviors and attitudes that we must continuously improve on, but our inborn aptitude is who we are. The Myers-Briggs Type Indicator (MBTI) is a valuable tool for assessing and understanding our inborn personality—why we do the things we do, why certain tasks are so easy for us while others are so difficult, and why we so easily connect with those similar to ourselves and are irritated by those who are not.

I recently read an article from Prof. Adam Grant, where he disagrees with the science behind the Myers-Briggs theory and calls it "mesearch instead of research". I added a chapter at the end adding my own positive experience with the MBTI and my "mesearch". In addition, one should never rely on one mode of evaluation rather using multitudes of techniques and tools, many that I explain in detail in the following chapters.

Let's try a simple test: Take a pen and paper and sign your name. Now switch hands and sign again. Most people say they can't, and the ones who try find it very awkward. Our inborn personality, our aptitude, is the dominant hand that writes naturally.

This dominant personality is called our aptitude. The MBTI measures this aptitude based on four sets of opposite polarities, and it assigns a letter to each extreme. There are sixteen different possible combinations, and most everyone falls into one of these sixteen types.

The polarities are:

Extrovert (E) vs. **Introvert** (I), which determines where a person derives their energy from (e.g., are you more comfortable being with people (E), or would you rather have quiet time (I)?)

Sensing (S) vs. **iNtuition** (N), which looks at how people take in information and what we trust more (e.g., do you trust more your five senses (S), or do you trust more your intuition or "6th sense"?)

Thinking (T) vs. **Feeling** (F), which is how we make our decisions. (e.g., to make a decision) do you use logic (T), or do you use feelings, your own or others, to make your decision (F)?.

Judging (J) vs. **Perceiving** (P), which describes how we might organize our life (e.g., are you naturally organized and enjoy schedules (J), or do you enjoy being more flexible and open ended with as many options as possible (P)?)

The Judging vs. Perceiving personalities are also used to describe our dominance as apparent to others. So, if you are more Judging, and your decision-making process is more visible, then you tend towards the J polarity, which is being organized. If people instead see more of how you take in information, then you tend towards the polarity of P, which is flexibility.

I'll give you an example of one set of polarities: Let's say two people go to a wedding. After a while, one says to the other, "It's so noisy. I'm ready to go home," while the other says, "Where are we running? I'm just starting to enjoy myself."

What's the difference between these two people?

When I ask this question at seminars, most people answer that one is a "schmoozer" and the other is antisocial. But those are behaviors, not inborn aptitudes. What it boils down to is that one is an introvert (represented by an I on the MBTI) while the other is an extravert (or E). The most important difference between the two is how and where they get their energy. Extraverts are energized by being with many people, while introverts lose energy when they find themselves in a crowd, and they feel the need to retreat to a quiet place to reenergize. E's usually have many friends but not necessarily deep friendships, while the I's have lesser friends but more deep relationships.

In the book *Please Understand Me* Dr. David Keirsey (1921-2013), a noted Professor and Psychologist, has clustered the sixteen types of the MBTI into four basic temperaments: the artisan, the guardian, the rational, and the idealist. Each temperament has its own unique qualities and shortcomings, strengths and challenges. The four temperaments spring from an interaction of the two basic dimensions of human behavior: our communication and our action, our words and our deeds—or simply, *what we say* and *what we do*.

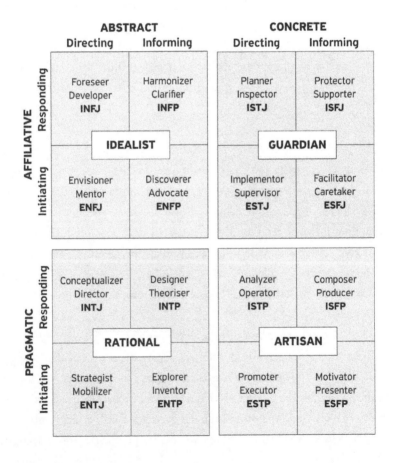

What We Say:
People naturally talk about what interests them. Some talk about concrete facts and figures, what has to be done, and how to do it. They talk about news, weather, sports, family, and their job. Others talk about abstract ideas: their hopes and dreams, their thoughts, and their philosophies. Obviously, most people talk about both. But the question is what do they enjoy? What do they feel comfortable talking about primarily?

What We Do:
The next question is how we go about our business: Some people do what gets results. They work as efficiently as possible to get to where they need to go. Others act primarily based on what's good for *everyone*, not necessarily putting themselves above anyone else. If it's not fair to others, they don't do it. They try to do the right thing, as agreed upon by a civil and polite society. These two customs can overlap, and most people act both ways at one time or other. But the question is, what do you do *most* of the time? What is your natural instinct?

What We Are:
According to Keirsey, you will find yourself in a specific corner of the chart based on what you talk about and what you tend to do. If you talk hard facts and play fair with others, you're a *Guardian*. If you talk hard facts and go for the goal, you're an *Artisan*. If you enjoy talking about ideas and then going through with them, no matter the cost, you're a *Rational*. And if you talk ideas and then play fair, you're an *Idealist*.

 Guardians, or *SJs*, are the pillars of society.

- They mostly speak about their duties.
- They have a natural talent for managing goods and services.
- They obey the laws and follow the rules.
- They pride themselves on being hard-working and dependable.
- They are cautious about change, and meticulous about schedules.

- They use their skills to help others. They keep things running smoothly in their family life, business life, and in their communities as well.
- They trust authority, join groups, and seek security—or provide it.
- They make stabilizing leaders who tend to be concerned with instituting rules and making sure everyone follows them. Many become supervisors, inspectors, or protectors. They also make responsible parents and loyal mates.

Artisans, or *SPs*, love working with their hands, and they seem right at home with tools, instruments, and vehicles of all kinds. They "Just do it."

- They want to be where the action is. They constantly seek out pleasure and stimulation, and feel that anything that is not pleasurable or stimulating is a waste of time.
- They speak mostly about what they see in front of them and are mostly focused on the here and now.
- They pride themselves on being bold, new, and spontaneous. They don't want to be tied down or confined.
- They possess the ability to excel in the arts, as well as in the art of making deals, and the art of excelling in the political arena.
- They are extremely competitive. They will do whatever it takes to accomplish their goals, even if they have to bend the rules or redefine them.
- They make good, trouble-shooting leaders who tend to go with the flow of the moment and are not too particular with creating or following rules. Many become performers, composers, or promoters.

Idealists, or *NFs*, try to reach their hopes and dreams without compromising their ethics.

- They speak mostly of their ideas and what they hope for.
- They try to avoid conflict and confrontation. Many actively take a role in which they can convince others to do the same, and they create harmonious, cooperative relationships.
- They are passionately concerned about personal growth and are naturally drawn to working with people for the good of all. They love to help others find their way in life.
- They believe the best way to reach goals is through meaningful cooperation and being one's best possible self.
- They are highly ethical and won't compromise themselves at all, and they hope for the same in others. When they do compromise their ethics, they are especially disappointed in themselves.
- Idealists make nurturing parents and inspirational leaders who tend to focus on how their work is changing the world, and having people buy into the mission is extremely important. Many also become teachers, counselors, or healers.

Rational's, or *NTs*, are problem solvers.

- They speak of problems that intrigue them and of issues they have with the complex systems that make up the world around us. They are particularly interested in the abstract concepts that underlie all systems.
- They try to figure things out and make them better, or, if need be, get around them.
- They act as effectively as possible to accomplish their goals, often ignoring rules, conventions, and everyone else if they have to.
- They are independent, strong-willed, and logical, but because of their absorbed concentration on the matter at hand, may be seen as cold and distant by others.
- They value intelligence above all else, and they pride themselves on their ingenuity.

- They don't care about being politically correct or about customary procedures they're supposed to follow. What matters is that they must accomplish their goals, and they work tirelessly on any project they set their mind to.
- Their levelheadedness and eye-on-the-prize mentality makes them very effective, strategic leaders who are concerned with making change happen, even at the cost of stepping on some of those that don't go along. Many become CEOs, inventors, or field marshals.

This is just a brief overview of the four basic temperaments to give you a very basic idea of the reasons behind the different behaviors we tend to observe in people. Humans are very complex, however, so four archetypes are not enough to capture the diversity of human behavior. These four temperaments are a good starting point for understanding what leadership skills you inherently possess so that you can build on them and become a successful manager.

Can aptitude be good or bad? It's neither. It's who we are. We may encounter circumstances where we practice one over the other. For example, as a boss we might need to fire people, even though by nature we are soft hearted. But there is no real need to change who we are. Though many times, people have a very hard time changing their nature. There are bosses that cannot fire people even though they know it's the right thing. Another example might be if we are not that organized but understand that in different situations like organizing a family or business event, its important to be well planned and well organized. I've suggested to many leaders that are not by nature organized to just hire the most competent and organized assistant and delegate to them those tasks that require structure and order.

Then there are problems that can result from different aptitudes that can be irritating to the other. We look at other personalities and can't understand them. For example, the I's feel that the E's are too talkative, too intrusive, and are poor listeners. (An Introvert that I knew once said that the Extrovert talks even when he doesn't have anything to say.) The E's think that the I's are too secretive, play very close to the vest and are the last to speak up. S's look at the N's as dreamers or pie in the sky types, while N's look at S's as very narrow minded and too literal. The T's might look at the F's as being overly sensitive and too emotional, while the F's see the T's as being cold and calculated without heart. Most probably the J's and the P's have the most problems. As the J's see the P's as sloppy, unorganized and unreliable while the P sees the J as rigid, too structured and inflexible.

In businesses and organizations, differences affect managers and employees alike.

One boss I coached would, at the end of each day, call in his managers as a group and socialize with them. He believed that he was building great relationships, but he didn't realize that the introverted managers in his team were drained by this. So it took him understanding his own aptitude for communication as well as that of others to alter his management style to a way that suits his entire team. Now he has learned to ask if they want to stay and schmooze instead of thrusting all of his people into social situations that make them uncomfortable.

By first understanding our own preferences and then understanding other people's preferences, we can ask them, for example, if they enjoy working with a lot of other people in an open space (which E's like), or if they prefer an enclosed space, (which I's prefer). As a leader, do you want your people to be practical and concrete, or do you enjoy them being big-picture and out-of-the-box thinkers (S's are more concrete while N's are more big-picture thinkers)? Are you more concerned with being liked or respected (F's like to be liked; T's want to be respected)? Does your work environment need to be highly organized, or do you tolerate some disorder (J's like order; P's will tolerate some messiness)?

Understanding others and ourselves goes a long way toward working with people and understanding how to utilize each person's strengths and abilities. The trick, according to Jim Collins in *Good to Great*, is "to put the right person in the right seat on the right bus." Making sure you understand the strengths of your people will allow you to help them be in the right place and achieve greater success.

Former General Electric Chairman and CEO, Jack Welch, named "Manager of the Century" by *Fortune* Magazine, had a very simple, yet clever model for evaluating his people. Welch, who was known for being a particularly brilliant leader when it came to developing talent, constantly raised the bar throughout his many years at the helm of the company. In order to continually improve on the quality of his people, he employed something that became known as his "A," "B," "C" model.

"A" Players are passionate individuals who execute successfully while living the values of the organization. These people represent the very best in any organization—which is why they get promoted more quickly than all others in a company.

"B" Players are those that live the values of the company but for some reason do not execute well. They might miss their sales number or fall short in other measurable ways. However, Welch felt strongly that anyone who lived the values of the company deserved another chance, so he often moved "B" players into different jobs or gave them new assignments.

"C" Players do not execute, and they do not live the values of the company. For "C's" the decision was easy for Welch. He would fire anyone who fit into this category. These are the people who often make up the bottom ten percent of any organization.

Since I never had the privilege of running a multinational company like General Electric, I rely on a different model that is quite useful in evaluating different leadership and management personalities. It is not as simple as Welch's "A," "B," "C," model, yet it has been proven to work on a grander scale for people at every level of any size organization. Kiersey in his bestselling book(s) Please Understand Me 1&2, defines the different types and their management styles.

I have found the Rational's or the iNtuitive Thinkers (NT's) to be the very best leaders, as they combine big vision with great execution. This is probably what Welch would call an "A" player. My father was a Rational (NT) as he had big visions and great executions. I would guess that Jack Welch is a Rational (NT) leader himself! (Kiersey's site says the same).

The Idealists or the iNtuitive Feelers (NF's) have a great sense of purpose and mission, yet they need to learn how to overcome their feelings and make the tough decisions. The Guardians or the Sensing Thinkers (ST's) have great executing skills but need to learn how to think big picture and utilize their intuition more. Welch might call them the "B" players.

The Artisans or Sensing Thinkers (STP's) have a hard time with keeping to the vision and executing well. The same goes for the SFP's. They might be the "C" players.

Myers-Briggs has recently introduced MBTI 2, which is more detailed version of the regular MBTI and it divides each of the 4 types into 5 additional types. I highly recommend using this version as its much more accurate and revealing. It also allows for better understanding of the differences within the 4 types. For example: In E vs. I there are additional 5 differences. Initiating vs. Receiving, Expressive vs. Contained, Gregarious vs. Intimate, Active vs. Reflective, Enthusiastic vs. Quiet. The same is for the other types.

At a recent leadership-training seminar, I presented a lecture on the different types of aptitudes, and we did a Myers-Briggs test on all the participants. The results gave people great insight into their management personality. One educational leader commented that when he took the test, he was amazed at how "it accurately portrayed [his] own personality to the T." The test allowed him to identify and understand many problem areas in his life, such as how, for example, as an introvert, he needed extra energy to mingle with people at conventions. Also, in meetings he would first listen to what everyone else had to say, as opposed to others, who could just freely speak their mind, which meant that he often lost the opportunity to participate in the discussion. However, as an iNtuitive Thinker, he loved solving the world's educational problems.

The MBTI is accurate for over 75 percent of the people who take it (and in fairness to the test, not everyone answers all the questions honestly). There are many levels of each type, and most people are not one extreme or the other. In general, results are typically an even split between the different personalities. So there is a great chance that you will encounter and have to work closely with someone different than you.

I highly encourage managers to do what all the larger companies and organizations do, which is administer an MBTI to all prospective hires in order to have a clear understanding of each person's strengths and abilities and to make sure that the job you're hiring them for doesn't go against their very nature. In addition, you can use the different types—for example, the extraverts who say what's on their minds and the introverts who stand back and listen before reacting—to create and enhance teamwork. For example, I have created the two-minute rule. Extraverts can only speak for two minutes, and Introverts must speak for two minutes. This allows both types to hear each other and not irritate each other. Or have them coach each other on their respective strengths. The MBTI is a great tool for accomplishing both.

I highly recommend using the MBTI test by going to http://www.myersbriggs.org/my-mbti-personality-type/take-the-mbti-instrument.

While I'm by far not a Professor, never mind a Wharton Professor like Adam Grant, I'd like to share my understanding of the usefulness and importance of Aptitude testing such as Myers-Briggs and Kiersey. Most other tests, including those that Prof. Grant is advocating are, as far as I understand, attitude or behavior tests. Those are hugely beneficial and in later chapters I refer to other tests such as Emotional Intelligence, Positive or Negative thinking, etc. The Aptitude test is more of "Why" we do things vs. "How" we do things. Most people never explore deeply enough, why we do the things we do, why we study the things we study, why we enjoy certain jobs and why we don't enjoy other jobs and the list goes on.

When I first came across these tests they were very revealing as to why I do certain things and why I don't do other things. For example, I was very interested in building Leadership, bigger picture thinking, mission statements, etc. These are directly attributable to my Rational (NT) type. Adam and I share this trait, though I always tested this way.

I am also an Ambivert (E&I mid zone), which allows me to enjoy people yet escape to my corner when I need to. I was never shy but had to work hard on getting over stage fright and now I speak publicly at ease. I wouldn't give up MBTI just yet.

Chapter 2

NATURE VS. NURTURE VS. CHOICE: Which One Is Right?

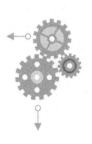

"*Never confuse efforts for results.*"
—**Barry Engel**

I f we are to be a leader, we need to think about the following: Are we predetermined by our nature and cannot possibly change who we are? Or are we solely the product of the society and the environment in which we grew up? Or do we have options? If so, what are they, and how can we apply them to our management and leadership style? I recently attended a seminar by a noted psychologist who stated that according to recent studies "Genetics [nature] make up about 50% of who we are; the rest is determined by various factors like culture, education [nurture], and our choices."

Who we are is one of the oldest debates in our society. *Nature* refers to our innate or inborn qualities, and *nurture* refers to personal experiences or learned behaviors—for example, the way we were raised. The difference is highlighted in a quote attributed to psychologist Donald Hebb, who is said to have once answered a journalist's question of "Which, nature or nurture, contributes more to personality?" by asking in response, "Which contributes more to the area of a rectangle, its length or its width?"

Some philosophers, such as Plato and Descartes, suggested that certain aspects of our personality are inborn; they simply occur naturally, regardless of environmental influences. We all know that certain physical traits are determined, or at least influenced, by our genes, such as height, eye color, vulnerability to certain illnesses, and so on. This has led many to speculate as to whether certain psychological traits, such as tendencies, mental abilities, and personality tics, are inherited as well. For example, the Human Genome Project has stimulated enormous interest in tracing different types of behavior to specific strands of DNA.

Other well-known thinkers, such as John Locke, believed in what is known as *tabula rasa*, which suggests that the mind begins as a blank slate. According to this notion, everything that we are and all of our knowledge is determined by our experience. The way we are brought up (nurture) shapes the way we see the world.

So, with these two varying notions of inborn tendencies versus learned traits, if a person devotes her life to reaching out and helping people, is she doing so because of the environment in which she grew up, or because she is genetically predisposed to doing so? Most experts today believe that it's a combination of both factors. As it turns out, there is too much evidence in favor of both theories to totally accept one philosophy and ignore the other.

So then the question really becomes, "Yes, a person is influenced by both nature and nurture, but by which is he or she *more strongly* influenced? What is the percentage? 50/50? 60/40? 90/10?" This version of the question was framed by Francis Galton in the late 19th century.

On the other hand, in recent years there's been a growing realization that the question is not even as simple as that. Biology and upbringing aren't two separate factors, one of which creates certain traits and one of which creates others; every trait is created by a combination of both factors, and it is impossible to unravel each trait and decide how much of each one can be attributed to which factor.

But while this debate continues to rage, it's important that we realize that neither our genetic predisposition nor our experiences need shape our destiny. Not everything we do *can* be blamed, or *has* to be blamed, on the past. There is a third, more proactive option, and that is *choice*, or *free will*. (The classic discussion of free will appears in Maimonides, *Laws of Repentance*, chapters 5–6). In other words, we don't have to do what we're programmed to do.

Viktor Frankl, best known for his great book *Man's Search for Meaning*, who was a Jewish Austrian neurologist and psychiatrist as well as a Holocaust survivor, explained that we all have the ability and freedom to choose how to act and how to react to whatever happens to us, and that we're not just victims of circumstance. Frankl realized that even in such a horrendous place as a concentration camp he had a choice about how to live his life. He believed that the most important attribute that helped people survive was their belief that they could still influence their own lives and contribute to humanity. He himself would imagine lecturing in front of his students about all the difficult choices he had to make and how he was able to overcome these great challenges.

In *The 7 Habits of Highly Effective People*, Covey quotes Frankl and says that we are the product of our choices, And, quotes an unknown author, "between stimulus and response there is a space. In that space lies our freedom and power to choose our response. In those choices lie our growth and our happiness."

We frequently hear problems from people who seem to be victims of circumstance:

> *I've met my career goals and achieved professional success, but it has cost me my personal and family life. I don't know my wife and children anymore. I'm not even sure I know myself and what's really important to me.*
>
> *I expect a lot from my employees, and I work hard to be friendly and fair, but I don't feel any loyalty from them. I think if I were sick for a day, they'd spend most of their time gabbing at the water cooler. Why can't they be responsible?*
>
> *There's so much to do, and there's never enough time. I feel pressured and hassled—all day, every day. I don't feel that I'm living the happy, productive, peaceful life I want to live.*
>
> *I'm busy—really busy. But I wonder if what I'm doing will make any difference in the long run. I'd like to think that there is meaning to my life and that my contributions make a difference.*
>
> *I have a forceful personality. In almost any interaction, I can control the outcome and even influence others to come up with the solution I want. But I feel uneasy. I always wonder what other people really think of me and my ideas.*

These are deep, painful problems that quick-fix approaches can't solve. Most people look at how others should change first before they themselves will commit to change. For example, I could say that my boss needs to change first, and then that will change my reactions to him or her. The same goes with reacting to spouses, parents, children, teachers, and other potentially conflicted relationships in our lives. However, the truth is that the only person you have the control to change is yourself. You need to change first, and then look at how you can help influence others.

Jack Welch, once again of GE fame, felt that successfully influencing others was a vital part of effective leadership. In his "4E" leadership model, the second "E" was "energize." Energizers, he asserted, were those able to articulate a vision and get other people to carry it out. Covey had a different take on all of this. He calls this the inside-out approach: first start by changing yourself (your "inside")—your paradigms, character, motives, and reactions—to change those things on the outside that make you unhappy.

He lists five ways to accomplish this:

- If you want to be a happy person, be the kind of person who generates positive energy and sidesteps negative energy.
- If you want to have pleasant, cooperative children, be a more understanding, empathic, consistent, loving parent.
- If you want to have more freedom and more latitude in your job, be a more responsible, helpful, contributing employee.
- If you want to be trusted, be trustworthy.
- If you want the secondary greatness of public recognition, focus first on the primary greatness of character.

Changing your situation and relationships all about making a proactive choice. The question I suggest that people should ask themselves to stimulate proactive career or business thinking is, "If money were not an issue and I couldn't fail, what would I be doing?" Most people are where they are in life because of how they've reacted to a series of events and situations. The key is to find what fears and preconditioning are preventing them from being where they want to be.

Highly proactive people recognize their responsibility. They do not blame their circumstances, conditions, or conditioning for their behavior or actions. In Covey's definition, being proactive means accepting that as human beings we are fully responsible for our own lives. We have a responsibility for how we choose to act and make things happen. The behavior and actions of proactive people are the result of their conscious choices based on their values, rather than their feelings or conditions. Responsibility or "response-ability"? If we look at the word *response-ability*, we get a better understanding of what *responsibility* means. It is an ability to choose our response. With a proactive focus, we can change more than what we thought possible.

Reactive people are those who are constantly affected by their environment. When people are nice to them and treat them well, they feel good. When people give them a hard time, they feel grumpy. Similarly, if the weather is good, they are in a pleasant mood; if it's raining, it affects their performance and attitude. Proactive people, on the other hand, carry their own weather with them; they are not unduly influenced by outside forces. Instead they know what they want to accomplish, and by having a clear sense of purpose and mission they stay true to their convictions.

Dealing with difficult people can be quite challenging, but as Gandhi once said, "They cannot take away our self-respect if we do not give it to them." Or, in the words of Eleanor Roosevelt, "No one can hurt you without your consent."

Covey's belief that you always have a choice, no matter how bad it gets, is very difficult to accept emotionally, especially for those who get dealt very tough cards in life. Life is not fair, but no matter what, we still have a choice in how to respond. Imagine what changes you could make in your life if you embraced the concept of proactivity.

A good way to gauge how proactive you are is to look at the language you use when you talk to people, or even when you think about life.

Reactive Language

- There's nothing I can do.
- That's just the way I am.
- He makes me so mad.
- They will never allow that.
- I have to do that.
- I can't.
- I have to.
- If only.

Proactive Language
- Let's look at the alternatives.
- I can choose a different approach.
- I control my own feelings.
- I can create an effective presentation.
- I will choose an appropriate response.
- I choose.
- I prefer.
- I will.

Covey says that there are four special human endowments that give us the power of choice:

1. **Self-Awareness**: understanding that between the point of stimulus and the point of response, you do have a choice. Not every stimulus has only one possible response. If someone offers you a cookie, you can choose not to take it. If someone doesn't take your feelings into account, you can choose not to be insulted. We can't control how people act; we can only control how we react.

2. **Conscience**: Using your inner compass of what's wrong and right, decide on the best course of action in a given situation, despite what everyone else is doing. Remember what Drucker said: "Leadership is about doing the right thing."

3. **Creative Imagination:** Visualizing new, alternative responses to a given situation. Your knee-jerk reaction isn't always the best course to take. The story about Victor Frankl is based on his ability to visualize the better future.

4. **Independent Will**: Choosing your own unique response, without necessarily confirming to others' expectations.

Mary Kay Ash, the founder of the cosmetics company Mary Kay, is believed to have said, "There are three types of people: those that make things happen, those that watch things happen, and those that ask, 'What happened?'" Too many people are afraid to find their own voice. They just follow instead of lead. You need to know what you stand for and what you won't stand for. Ask yourself, what am I passionate about, why am I passionate about it, and how can I make a difference and then do it? Don't wait for others; make it happen!

My father liked to quote his accountant who said "Never confuse efforts for results".

It's also worth noting that sometimes, no matter how hard you try, you won't be able to change things. There is a 10/90 rule of life. Ten percent of things are out of your control, so choose to focus your energy on how to respond to them rather than control them. This is expressed well in the famous Serenity Prayer: "G-D, grant me the serenity to accept the things I cannot change, the courage to change the things I can, and the wisdom to know the difference."

Leaders need to know the difference between what they can change and what they can't.

Chapter 3

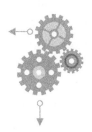

THE ASSERTIVE LEADER:
Are You Blunt or Bluff?

"Mean what you say, say what you mean, but don't say it mean."
(Unknown)

H ave you ever wondered how you communicate with your team and others? Passively? Aggressively? Or both?

Here's a story that illustrates the point:

Lee was generally happy with his job as manager in his company, yet he sometimes felt intimidated by his aggressive boss, Matt. He simply could not figure out how to resolve his feelings. He feared talking to Matt because he was intimidated by him. Instead, Lee would passively sulk and remain silent.

At the same time, Matt had thoughts of his own that he wished he could express to Lee. While generally satisfied with Lee's work, he wanted to share methods that would improve his productivity. Matt, however, did not know how to express his desire for Lee to improve while still conveying his appreciation of Lee as an employee; Lee's passivity made Matt feel that Lee didn't care enough about the business.

In addition, Matt had unrealistic optimism about how much business they would generate and what Lee could earn in terms of salary and commission. When sales were not what they both projected, Lee didn't feel fairly compensated, but he feared expressing these thoughts to Matt.

Through our assertive and leadership training, both Matt and Lee learned how to be assertive and were coached on how to express their concerns and issues without hurting or blaming the other.

"Now I finally know how to let Matt know how unappreciated I felt when I only heard complaints, never compliments," says Lee.

Matt is also thankful to finally have the tools to accept responsibility and provide honest and realistic feedback on accomplishments and what needs to improve. He says, "Instead of keeping my feelings of Lee needing to improve inside of me, I now have a way to sandwich my criticism in a complimentary way. I can't tell you how much more productive our meetings are. We're focusing so much more on results and future goals—without any bad feelings!"

Both Lee and Matt took responsibility for their own past communication mistakes. Today they have the tools to work together while expressing their own ideas. But more importantly, they know how to bring their own unique ideas into a shared vision for the future success of their company.

Achieving Assertiveness

We've all met aggressive people. They're the ones who cut to the chase, bluntly stating their agenda almost to the point of intimidation until their own personal goals are met. "You will do X until we reach a fifteen percent increase in revenues by year end," is a simple, yet curt example. Too many people believe that forceful and aggressive behavior is a necessary ingredient for financial success. That was a quality that Jack Welch forcefully fought against. He had no patience for bullies who simply barked out orders to his direct reports. He preferred a far softer approach.

The most successful and effective leaders that I have met have all had a softer approach. While they were not pushovers, they had the confidence and self-esteem to be open and honest, yet assertive, in communicating their and their organization's needs.

But what happens when a business deal is conducted between two aggressive people? Surely an enormous waste of energy is expended as each promotes an agenda in a tense atmosphere.

How about the passive type? They prefer not to express their opinions, ideas, and feelings because they fear it may rock the boat. They seem to have no opinion of their own and can be manipulated and controlled very easily. Passive people usually avoid saying no in order to be nice. They think the only alternative to being nice is to be mean or selfish. Recently, I was involved with an organization where the leadership was not happy with how the sales team ran their budgets. So, the manager would just shrug his shoulders whenever asked for an opinion. It was his passive way of disagreeing. A more functional manager would have assertively expressed his doubts and concerns. The problem went unaddressed for so long and became a big enough problem that the manager eventually "lost his cool." He yelled and pounded on the table, and in the process he alienated his salespeople.

Aggressive people enjoy being around passive people, because passives allow them to do their own thing in their own time in their own way, even if it involves manipulation and abuse. Passive people, meanwhile, take the path of least resistance. If someone takes advantage of them, they let it go.

Most passive people have a hard time with confrontation for one of two reasons:

1. They hate how it makes them feel. They hate the physiological changes that come with a tense situation, such as second-guessing themselves or losing their cool. And then, when they don't speak up and no one reads their minds, there is the additional frustration and helplessness that makes them feel even worse.

2. Many passive people have low self-esteem. They feel like no one can understand how they feel and that everyone is always taking advantage of them. They learn early on that the best way to get by is to say nothing and not stand out.

Then there is a third type of person—the passive-aggressive person. Passive-aggressive people are actually pretty aggressive on the inside, but they're very non-confrontational about it. They pretend they're not upset by something, but they will do things to sabotage what you're trying to do, directly or indirectly, still always leaving themselves the escape route of saying, "No, I didn't mean it that way. Boy, did you read too much into it." They don't directly express their feelings, but they show how they feel through what they do. And they're no easier to deal with than people who are directly aggressive. A husband and wife team that I worked with was confronted with this problem, where the husband would talk behind his wife's back about how she was making huge mistakes; rather than being open and honest, he would be passive in front of her and aggressive behind her back.

A Guide to the Things Passive-Aggressive People Say:

1. **"Fine. *Fine.*"** In other words, "I don't want to express my feelings. I'd rather sulk later."
2. **"Mad? I'm not mad. What makes you think I'm mad?"** That's pretty defensive. They might be mad.
3. **"I'll be there in five minutes."** Not every distance takes five minutes to traverse. Someone's trying to stall. Or even get out of something without directly refusing it.
4. **"Sure. No problem."** This is the equivalent of getting a form letter that says, "Thanks for your resume. We'll keep it on file." Maybe if they pretend they want to help you, you won't be upset when they don't. Right?
5. **"Oh. I thought you knew."** In other words, "I could have said something when I saw that your entire plan was about to take a nosedive. But I didn't wanna."
6. **"Oh. So everything has to be perfect."** There's a saying that if you do a good job, you're rewarded with more work. But if you make mistakes, no one will ask you to do it again. *Oh, you wanted it to be perfect? Well, maybe you should have done it yourself.*

7. **"That's pretty good for an amateur."** *That's not good. But considering you have no idea what you're doing, it's not as bad as I expected.* It's kind of like, "You look pretty good for your age."

8. **"What, you're offended?"** Now they turn it around. All of a sudden, *you're* the one trying to start the fight. They were being "helpful" all along. Boy, are *you* overreacting.

9. **"Gosh. I was just kidding."** Again, it's *your* fault that you took offense to something mean or inappropriate they said or did.

So the question is, how does a person avoid extremes in behavior and learn to clearly state his objective in a healthy, honest, and focused way, without hurting another's feelings or forcefully ruining a business deal?

The answer is *assertiveness*.

"Mean what you say, say what you mean, but don't say it mean." Clearly understand and believe in your own objectives so that you can be firm and outspoken in your ideas and positions. Assertiveness means being able to state your needs without feeling intimidated. It is the ability to stand up for yourself and to express how you feel when necessary. Assertiveness is an art worth learning; it will help you in all areas of your life. It may take a while getting used to, but once you master it, it is highly empowering.

Assertive people have some of the following characteristics:

- They feel free to express feelings, thoughts, and desires without feeling self-conscious.
- They are willing to compromise with others, rather than always wanting it their way.
- They have good self-esteem and are able to ask for what they want.
- They are able to say no to people without feeling guilty about it; they know their rights.
- They can choose how to live their life without feeling guilty about it.
- They are able to take risks when they feel they need to.

Assertive *leaders* are effective at the following:

- They are very clear and forthright about their organization's vision, mission, and goals.
- They are excellent communicators and great listeners.
- They are decisive and communicate their decisions.
- They hire great people, sometimes even better than themselves, and they delegate effectively.
- They hold themselves and their people accountable for results.
- They admit to mistakes and apologize when necessary.
- They love to learn and always add to their knowledge base.

Assertiveness is expressed by the word *I*, while the aggressive form tends to focus on the other person and is thus expressed as *you*. "Please allow me to share my concern" or "Let me tell you what's important to me" are expressions of assertiveness.

By assertively using the word *I*, you are saying, "I care enough to give you feedback." This is the most effective way to review the status of projects or tasks that the person is working on. If we are too intimidated or insecure to give feedback to others, how will they ever know our thoughts?

Some managers don't give honest feedback because they are afraid how their employees will react. Yet expressing feelings and opinions to others shows that we value that relationship. A manager can emphasize the positive while being careful to keep her productive feedback in the "I" voice instead of continually finger-pointing at her employees, accusing them of being the root of the company's problems.

Clearly expressing our needs in a non-confrontational manner while keeping the conversation focused on "I" as much as possible is almost a guarantee that others will be receptive to discussing the issue at hand.

Here are some examples of *I* vs. *you* statements:

I Statement	You Statement
I feel that…	You seem…
I'm concerned about…	You are messing up…
It's not working out…	It's your fault…
I am interested to hear why you think…	Your point of view is irrelevant.

Public Speaking: According to some, public speaking comes a close second to being in a Dentist's chair. Here are some important tips assertive people use to overcome the fear of public speaking:

It's important to speak with confidence *even if you don't feel confident*, practice speaking this way. Many years ago, I was part the Toastmasters speaking training, and they were very effective in helping people get over the fear of public speaking. I highly recommend their program. One of the more interesting things they taught us was called "Umm counting." Count how many times you or others say "Umm" during a speech. It's unprofessional. Learn how to pause instead of saying "Umm." A pause done correctly is a powerful addition to your speech. The Toastmasters required you to get up and speak. It was challenging at first, but slowly you get over the fear and start to concentrate on the things that make a good speaker.

The first time I had to give a major speech, I consulted with a speech coach. First I videotaped myself giving the speech, and we then reviewed it. I learned how to be a more effective presenter mostly by using positive body language that increased my confidence level. Learning presentation skills gives you confidence and it makes you a better speaker. Effective leaders will have positive body language, such as looking at the audience and not down at their notes. They will use open hand gestures, which shows openness, and not clench or hold their hands tightly. They sometimes will move to the front of the podium to show connection with their audience, or they will move around and not stand like a stiff board, which makes them seem very distant and hard to relate to.

The more you practice the more it will become second nature. Consider the times when you really wanted to stand up for yourself but felt you couldn't, or when you really wanted to say no but said yes, or when you didn't say anything when the jerk at work made you look like a fool.

One of the best ways to develop assertive traits in you is to observe them in others. Look at someone you admire. Most of the time you admire someone because that person has some kind of trait that you're lacking in your own life, a trait you wish you had, like assertiveness or confidence. Pay attention to how they do things, watch their body language, and take notes.

There may be some situations in which you find yourself acting aggressively and others that cause you to become passive. Ask yourself some questions to determine your triggers: Are there certain people you have the most problems with? Where does it occur most often? Is it harder for you to give compliments or to give criticisms—or are both difficult for you? Answering these questions will help you understand when and with whom problems with assertiveness arise.

A good way to increase your assertiveness skills is to practice different scenarios in your mind. Think of what you are going to say, what you want to say, and how you are going to say it, and then put it into practice. If you haven't done this before, it might take some time getting used to, but eventually it will become second nature. The following example of Robert demonstrates how this method of practicing for different scenarios can be extremely beneficial, not only for professional wellbeing, but for personal happiness as well.

Robert plans for almost all eventualities. He rehearses what might happen in certain situations, and he thinks about his response to it before it happens. He has developed a quick wit and assertiveness, and it's often amazing to see how people respond to him. He claims that in some situations he still finds it hard, but he has the right tools to do it anyway.

For example, Robert was at a seminar with many people, all of whom were qualified doctors, academics, senior practitioners, and so on. He was dying to ask the speaker a question to clarify something, but he felt it might be a silly question. He thought about it for a moment and decided to ask anyway. He rehearsed exactly what he was going to say, along with his tone and hand gestures, and he waited for the right moment to ask the question.

He says that as silly as it sounds, it felt very empowering. If he hadn't asked the question, he would have berated himself all day for not doing so. This is what being assertive is all about; it's not about being aggressive, a smart aleck, or whatever else; it's about knowing you have the right to ask a question or to stand up for yourself.

Once you have practiced and feel comfortable with what you are going to say, here are some tips to help you along:

- Keep your words straight and to the point; don't complicate it.
- Be polite but firm with the other person.
- Let everything the other person says wash over you and remain calm.
- Look the other person in the eye, but don't stare at him.
- Don't apologize if it's not necessary.

One last note of caution: Even though assertiveness is a wonderful skill to use in many situations, you still need to know when to pick your battles. Sometimes it's wiser to just let things wash over you. Leaders know when to hold and when to fold. Be careful in not needing to have the last word—that is aggressiveness. Sometimes you can agree to disagree, but never be disagreeable.

Chapter 4

EMOTIONS AND INTELLIGENCE:
Do They Go Together?

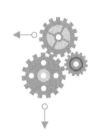

"Squash the ANTs (automatic negative thinking)."
—Jacob Engel

W arren Buffett was once asked about the most important quality a person needs in order to be successful in business. His answer was *emotional stability*.

If you look around, you'll realize that it is not necessarily the smartest people who are the most successful or the most fulfilled in life. You probably know people who are academically brilliant and yet are socially inept and unsuccessful at work or in their relationships. Intellectual intelligence, or IQ, isn't enough to make you successful. IQ can help you get into college, but it's your EQ, or emotional "quotient," or intelligence, that will help you manage the stress of sitting through your final exams.

Daniel Goleman, who popularized the concept of emotional intelligence, shows that being book-smart, or having IQ, is important, but being people-smart, having EQ, is a predictor of success. Goleman views EQ as an array of emotional and social competencies. Others define it as the ability to identify, understand, and manage emotions as well as possessing skills to regulate and harness emotions in order to achieve desired goals. Leaders are the most effective when they are using their EQ at its best. Understanding their employee's emotions is very powerful. Not getting too emotional (except when needed) is a huge skill that leaders need to practice. Employees look to their leaders to remain calm and collected, especially in very trying circumstances.

Today there are many theories and tests to explain and measure EQ, but it can be boiled down to four basic attributes:

- **Self-awareness:** You have the ability to recognize your own emotions and how they affect your thoughts and behavior; you're aware of your strengths as well as your weaknesses.
- **Social awareness:** You understand the emotions, needs, and concerns of other people. You're able to pick up on emotional cues and feel socially comfortable.
- **Self-management:** You are capable of managing your emotions in healthy ways, take initiative, follow through on commitments, and adapt to changing circumstances.
- **Relationship management**: You know how to develop and maintain good relationships, communicate effectively, inspire and influence others, and work well in a team.

Unlike your IQ, your EQ affects all areas of your life. It affects your career and performance level at work, and it helps you navigate the social complexities of the workplace. In fact, when it comes to screening job candidates, many companies now view emotional intelligence as equally important to technical ability and require EQ testing before hiring.

Emotional intelligence greatly affects your physical and mental health. If you're unable to manage your stress levels, it can lead to serious health problems. Uncontrolled stress can raise blood pressure, suppress the immune system, increase the risk of heart attack and stroke, and speed up the aging process. Stress also makes you vulnerable to anxiety, depression, and mood swings. Therefore, the first step to improving emotional intelligence is to learn how to relieve stress.

By understanding your emotions and how to control them, you're better able to express how you feel and to understand how others feel. This allows you to communicate more effectively and forge stronger relationships, both at work and in your personal life.

If emotional intelligence is so important to leading a successful life, how does a person go about developing it?

The key is being able to connect to your emotions of anger, fear, frustration, and sadness and understand how they affect your thoughts and actions. You can try to ignore those feelings, but you can't eliminate them. They're still there, and if you deny that they are, you're ignoring your own subconscious motivating factors.

When we're placed in a stressful situation, such as a tense meeting or a tight deadline, our instinct takes over, and our free will and ability to act thoughtfully are limited. You need to be able to control the emotional side of your brain to continue to function as you would in a stress-free environment. Simply reading about managing stress won't help; you need to be proactive and develop techniques of dealing with it in everyday life. If you're not used to being in touch with your emotions, it might be uncomfortable, draining, or feel like just a waste of time. But if you're aware of *why* you do the things that you do, of what influences your thoughts and actions, you can better try to steer them toward your end goals so you don't sabotage yourself. You can learn how to counteract that stress and calm yourself down so you don't let your emotions get the better of you, no matter how stressful the situation.

Step 1: Learn what stress feels like. Pay attention to what your body does when you're stressed. Do you suddenly start binge eating? Do you lose your appetite? Do your muscles tense up? Do your palms sweat? Once you know how your body reacts to stress, you can use those signs as early warnings to do something to combat that stress.

Step 2: Combat stress. If stressful situations make you angry or agitated, do something to sooth yourself. If you're a visual person, step outside and take in a view. If you're an auditory person, listen to your tunes or some beach noises. On the other hand, if stressful situations make you become withdrawn or depressed, you need to do something to stimulate your creativity and lighten the mood. Play a game or take in some comedy. In fact, a good hearty laugh elevates the mood, lowers blood pressure, reduces stress, and helps you see creative approaches to your situation.

Step 3: Be proactive about it. Set aside time every day to do something you enjoy—to laugh, to play, or to relax. It might seem like a waste of time that you don't have, but it will mitigate the stress of the rest of the day.

Once you have a handle on your EQ and know how to stay calm, stay present, and use humor and creativity, you will also be able to deal with emotional conflict, both at work and at home. You'll realize that in any relationship between two people, there are bound to be disagreements. You can't agree on *everything*. But the key is not to let disagreements become emotional. Having a handle on your EQ will help you catch and diffuse issues before they get worse, and it will help you to not hold onto old arguments and keep bringing them up. And if it's a conflict that can't be resolved, you will see that too. It takes two to argue, so you must learn to agree to disagree and move on.

Another focus of emotional intelligence is resiliency, or the ability to bounce back after a setback. While coaching entrepreneurs and managers over the years, we have found that this capability is very important to success. For example, an entrepreneur we trained said that after attending a resiliency seminar, he realized how important it was for him to learn this skill in order to bounce back from feelings of failure and move on to more productive things.

Most people aren't aware of the negative thinking that goes on in their minds—especially the fear of failure, which can lead to a whole train of negative thoughts. Dr. Daniel Amen calls this ANT: Automatic Negative Thinking. We say, "Squash the ANTs." Dr. Martin Seligman (see chapter 21), the father of Positive Psychology, suggests using the ABCDE Model, which Drs. Albert Ellis and Aaron Beck designed for Cognitive Behavior Therapy (CBT) as a way to counter negative thinking.

Adversity, Beliefs, Consequences, Dispute, Evidence. In other words, when we encounter an adverse situation that causes us stress, we should check out our thinking or beliefs associated with the event, as well as the consequences we believe will happen, and then dispute it with evidence.

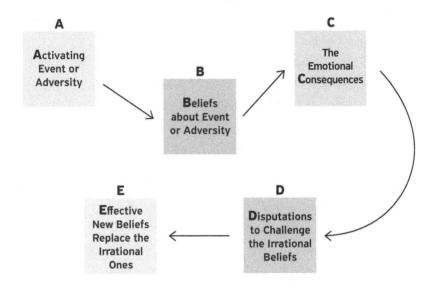

Let's look at an example:

A large client asks for an unexpected meeting. Immediately, you start to think, "Oh no! What did I do wrong?" (Adversity). "I bet he's going to drop his account" (Belief). After that, your thoughts start rolling out of control: "I probably won't be able to find another customer, and then I won't be able to pay my bills, my mortgage, or the kids' tuition, and then I'm going to lose my house. My kids will get thrown out of school, and they won't have anywhere to go home to" (Consequences).

Negative thinking is a behavior that can and should be reversed, or it can paralyze us in every aspect of our lives. The way to do that is by *disputing* with *evidence*. For example, you can tell yourself, "Clients have wanted to meet with me before, for various reasons. This is not the first time. And not one of those times did I lose an account." While it's good to always prepare for the worst, remember that 95 percent of the things we worry about never happen. Just remain calm and see what the client wants.

Once a manager learns how to manage stress internally, it is then their responsibility to manage the stress of their employees. Perhaps, as in the example above, your team finds out that a large client has asked for an unexpected meeting. One team member asks you what you think the team has done wrong, and another wonders to you whether you think the client is going to drop the account. You hear panicked mumblings throughout the office, of employees worried about the worst-case scenario for the meeting. As their manager, you must take the initiative to dispute the evidence for them to get your team back in working order. Just as you can't function when you're under stress, a team cannot work together if they are all distracted by the same pressure. An effective manager will call a staff meeting to prepare for the client's arrival, and he or she will begin the meeting by confronting the worries that have been plaguing the office. Cite other instances of similar meetings, and acknowledge to each one of your team members how they contributed to a past success in a stressful situation. Get your team back on track to remain calm and focus on what they need to do.

Dean Becker, who designs resilience courses and tests based on a great book, *The Resiliency Factor* by psychologists Karen Reivich and Andrew Shatté, explains that resiliency is a muscle in the brain that needs to be exercised. There are seven essential ingredients of resilience:

- **Emotion regulation:** Keeping your emotions in check
- **Impulse control:** Keeping your behavior in check
- **Causal analysis:** Diagnosing and solving problems effectively
- **Self-efficacy:** Belief in your ability to handle situations that come your way
- **Realistic optimism:** Belief in a bright future, but within the bounds of your reality
- **Empathy:** Identifying what motivates others
- **Reaching out:** Seeking out new opportunities, challenges, and relationships

Being resilient comes down to understanding the thoughts that precede our emotions and being able to change the underlying thinking—to cut off those thoughts before they turn into emotions. Becker says that all of our negative emotions are triggered by underlying thoughts that precede them, and we should be on the lookout for the following:

- **Anger:** "Someone violated my rights."
- **Frustration:** "I'm not getting the resources that I need."
- **Anxiety:** "Future threats are just around the corner."
- **Sadness:** "I lost something I thought I'd still have."
- **Guilt:** "I violated others' rights."
- **Embarrassment:** "I lost face."
- **Shame:** "I violated my own rules."

Once we can isolate these thoughts, we can learn how to replace them with positive thinking. For example, with anger, you can ask who said that those rights were yours, or with anxiety you can adopt a wait-and-see attitude before envisioning bad things happening.

In today's society we treasure happiness and positive thinking. Leaders must have the ability to enhance their own thinking and others' as well. Unhappy leaders will make unhappy employees, which make for unhappy clients. Authors like Seligman in *Authentic Happiness, The Optimistic Child*; Tal Ben Sahar in *Happier*; and others have written much about positive thinking. It is a skill that can be learned. I recently trained for certification as a Coach in Positive Psychology with Robert Biswas-Diener and found that there are a great many tools that are available in developing the positive mindset. The most usable tool that can be used even on your own is the strengths evaluation. Peter Drucker said "to achieve results, one has to use all available strengths…" Here are 3 simple yet powerful questions that Robert Diener says you can ask yourself.

1. What are some of the things in your past that makes you especially proud?

2. What energizes you in the present?
3. What are you looking for in the near future?

There are also tests that help identify strengths. Some of the well know ones are VIA (viacharachter.org) and Realise2-Capp (Cappeu.com). Many people don't focus on strengths because social norms dictate that we retain some modesty. We are not aware of our strengths. We often believe that we need to focus on improving our weaknesses, as that is our greatest area of growth.

Why are we then unhappy? The great Jewish philosopher Bahya ben Joseph ibn Paquda was the author of the first Jewish system of ethics, written in Arabic in 1080 under the title *Al Hidayah ila Faraid al-Qulub* (*Guide to the Duties of the Heart [Mind]*). He says that the source of most unhappiness is "jealousy," meaning that we are always looking at what others have and that there will always be someone wealthier, better looking, more competent, etc. than how we view ourselves. Or the lack of "attitude of gratitude," meaning that we don't count our blessings and are focused on what we don't have, or that we believe there is not enough to go around, and if someone else has something, it's as if it was taken from us. Covey calls the third one the "scarcity mentality," or the belief that there isn't enough to go around, not enough business, not enough money, not enough success, and so on. This idea is in conflict with the "abundance mentality," that there is plenty to go around, and the more win-win scenarios we create, the more we gain.

Once we isolate our thoughts and realize that our frustration is coming from this belief, we can work to instead adopt an abundance mentality—that is, that where this is coming from, there's a lot more for all. A good way to look at this is by comparing it to the pizza *pie* versus pizza *parlor* mentality. Everyone talks about making it in business as "getting a slice of the pie," and we tend to look at it that way. But if you look at pizza as coming from a pie, then every slice someone else has is one less slice that *you* can have. The key is to realize that every slice actually comes from a pizza *parlor*. In other words, there are plenty more pies where that one came from, so there's enough for everyone to find success.

Prosperous leaders are the ones who believe and help their people believe in abundance and that there is enough for everyone. They help them overcome their ANTs (automatic negative thinking) and replace it with positive thoughts and outcomes. They will inspire and motivate others to do the right thing, as this is the epitome of abundance mentality. They encourage teamwork, sharing of resources, and collaboration, as this is according to Ray Cammarano the hallmark of a prosperous organization (See Foreword).

I recently saw an article in the Harvard Business Review about a survey of what people think are the best leadership model.

In 2009, James Zenger published a fascinating survey of 60,000 employees to identify how different characteristics of a leader combine to affect employee perceptions of whether the boss is a "great" leader or not.

Two of the characteristics that Zenger examined were results focus and social skills. Results focus combines strong analytical skills with an intense motivation to move forward and solve problems. But if a leader was seen as being very strong on results focus, the chance of that leader being seen as a great leader was only 14%. Social skills combine attributes like communication and empathy. If a leader was strong on social skills, he or she was seen as a great leader even less of the time — a paltry 12%.

However, for leaders who were strong in both results focus and in social skills, the likelihood of being seen as a great leader skyrocketed to 72%!

This is emotional intelligence at its best.

PART 2

WHAT HOLDS US BACK:
The Problems and Solutions

Chapter 5

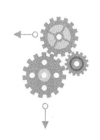

THE GREAT BALANCING ACT:
Prosperous Leaders at
Work and Home

*"No one ever said on their deathbed:
'I wish I'd spent more time at the office"*
—Harold Kushner

A man in the woods was struggling to saw down a tree. An old farmer came by, watched for a while, and then quietly asked, "What are you doing?"

"Can't you see?" the man replied impatiently, "I'm sawing down this tree!"

"You look exhausted," said the farmer. "How long have you been at it?"

"Over five hours, and I'm beat," the man replied. "This is hard work."

"That saw looks pretty dull," said the farmer. "Why don't you take a break for a few minutes and sharpen it? I'm sure it would go a lot faster."

"I don't have time to sharpen the saw," the man replied emphatically. "I'm too busy sawing!"

Stephen Covey uses this story to explain why, in order to maintain our most important asset—ourselves—we need to maintain a balance between the following four dimensions:

1. **The physical dimension (D1)**: our bodies. Maintaining this dimension involves eating right, exercising, and getting enough rest.
2. **The spiritual dimension (D2)**: our "center," or system of values. To maintain this dimension, we draw upon the sources that inspire us, uplift us, and tie us to the timeless truths of life.
3. **The mental dimension (D3)**: our minds. To keep this dimension sharp, we read, learn new things, and expose ourselves to great minds. Some mental exercises, such as organizing and planning, also help us maintain this dimension.
4. **The social/emotional dimension (D4)**: our emotional life and our relationships with other people. Maintaining our social/emotional dimension requires focus and exercise in our interaction with others.

To maintain a healthy balance, we must keep up on all four aspects of our lives. If we neglect any one area, it can impact everything else, including the other three dimensions. The four dimensions are legs on which a tabletop rests, piled with everything we have going on. If one leg is missing, the table will collapse. If one leg is shorter than the others, everything will eventually slide off.

In businesses and organizations, we use the same four dimensions to make sure that what we build is well balanced and successful for the long term. A *prosperous leader* will make sure that these four dimensions are in check in his or herself as well as within the organization.

The first (physical) is economic health or financial health. We need to make sure we have a positive cash flow and good profit margins, and that we can get banks to lend us money when needed. This is the lifeblood of success.

The second dimension (spiritual) is our mission and values. What is the purpose of our organization, what values are important to us, and how does that impact the people we work with? In other words, what *do* we stand for, and what *won't* we stand for? Jack Welch was one of the first CEOs of a *Fortune* 500 Company to bring values into the workplace. Values became the centerpiece of his people strategy and how he made the really tough decisions of whom to hire, fire, and promote.

The third dimension (mental) is developing talent. Helping our people be successful means that *we* are successful. Someone once asked, "What if we train our people and then they leave for other companies?" The reply: "So, what's the other option? Not to train them and they stay?"

The fourth dimension (social/emotional) is having a culture of trust. What's our culture like? Do our people trust each other? Do they communicate effectively? Do we have great teamwork? Do we lead by example and make sure that trust is emphasized as part of our organizational values?

With relationships, slow is fast, and fast is slow. They require building trust, which, when done correctly, takes time. And while it takes time, trust is the number-one factor in building great relationships. Sean Covey in his book about the "speed of trust" points out how much more effective we are when we have built trust. Organizations and leaders will be able to achieve much more with a trusting culture than without

In our training and consulting, we often come across companies that are good on one or even a few of the four dimensions, but balance is lacking. And, on the individual level, many leaders and managers are overly stressed and haven't invested in the balance of their own *personal* four dimensions. Having a correct balance between the four dimensions of both our personal and business lives will benefit our companies and us. In Covey's story of the man sawing down the tree, he was worried about his time resources (physical), but he lost sight of his goal (spiritual). As a result, he was exhausted, working hard, not getting much done, and losing his patience.

As a business coach, I come across many individuals, both managers and leaders, who struggle with maintaining a healthy balance between their personal or family lives and their professional or work lives. Yet as Harold Kushner said, "No one ever said on their deathbed: "I wish I'd spent more time at the office". So how do we keep score of where we are over weighted on one or more dimensions and where we should be more balanced?

A great exercise is to ask the people close to you where they think you are in the four dimensions. Which areas do they think you have a solid foundation in, and which areas do they feel that you could use more focus? You can do this with your managers. Ask them how you rate, and ask them if they are interested in hearing your opinion about how they rate. So many times we think we are well balanced and that our families or coworkers are appreciative of all our efforts, when, in fact, they really think we are out of balance and need to have better equilibrium.

A great way to do this exercise in your personal life is to hold family meetings. They can be with as many people you wish to include. First, you will need to identify your family mission. Years ago, our family sat down with a facilitator and asked that we come together and create a family mission statement. It took us a better part of a day and we were able to create the values that we as a family will live by. It proudly hangs in my study. Another very effective person told me that he "inherited" an ethical will from his grandmother, which he and his family adopted as their own. It is now framed and hangs in their family room. (see chapter 9 for examples and suggestions in crafting your own mission statement)

Many companies and organizations will similarly do a 360-degree evaluation using, for example, the 7 Habits as an evaluation tool. It covers all four areas of effectiveness.

As a leader, it's important for the "main thing to be the main thing." So if you are focused on helping your managers and employees look at all four dimensions in their work and personal lives, they must understand that if it's important for you, it should be important for them.

Years ago I attended a seminar where the presenter posed the following question. He was the principal of a very large high school, and graduation was a big deal. It was his day, and he made sure that it was really exceptional for his students and staff. One year, however, his own child was to graduate, but in another school an hour away. His question was where should he attend—his school or his child's graduation? It became a hotly contested discussion, as some argued that his priority was with his students; others argued that his child was more important. He ended up going to both, and in his own words, he was neither here nor there. Now many years later when he reflects on it, he said that he realized that after his retirement, he was replaced, and his legacy was just a page in the graduation book. But he remained a father to his child all his life, and that was his true priority.

Recently in a seminar where I was doing a training session, David, the owner of a condo service, attended with his daughter. He told us that his challenge was that he, his wife, and all of his staff were working incredibly hard, and everyone felt stressed out. He felt he was close to burnout and couldn't continue. His question was whether he should sell the business or just work harder, as he didn't see any other option.

He confided when he came to our seminar that he was skeptical that anything could change, as, after all, he was working as hard as he could, and so was anyone else. But after learning about finding the balance between four dimensions, it was like a new world opened up for him. He learned how taking care of himself first would help his company grow economically (D1), how to train and empower his employees (including his daughter) (D3), how to step back and see where he would like the company to be in a few years (D2), and how to create an organization where he could trust his employees to be dependable (D4).

We helped him identify that, as a workaholic (a condition he was unaware of), he would take on whatever work wasn't being done by others. We helped him understand the powerful yet hard to implement principle of delegating responsibilities to his key people. His wife and daughter were highly competent and could do many of the jobs, but he believed that only he could make decisions, and they were reluctant to tell him that this was undermining their authority.

This is a very common problem that I see in our consulting work. People are very reluctant to tell someone else that they are treating them as "gofers" (go for this and go for that). However, if you treat your people this way, they will never step up to the plate. Why should they? If you want to make all the decisions and not include your key people in your decision-making process, they will let you work harder and harder, all the while waiting for you to fall or fail.

One of the effective ways to overcome this common problem is to create a list of the various responsibilities, and name that will be responsible for the results. Then you can delegate the responsibilities effectively and empower your people to take on new roles. Otherwise people don't feel empowered and will not be committed, as they will see themselves as just pushovers. (See chapter 12 for a more in-depth explanation.)

So, his personal goal was first and foremost to empower others to run the business on a day-to-day basis. He accomplished that by including his team in divvying up responsibilities and making sure that the distribution of labor was very clear and well thought out. His wife took on the role of customer service manager, and she became empowered to make decisions based on the understanding of what the company agreed to provide to the condo owners and what the company was capable of providing. This opened the avenue for a healthy dialogue between the condo owners and the service company. The owner's daughter was empowered to be responsible for all the financials. She then hired the accounting staff to help her avoid getting bogged down with data entry and other jobs that others could do. The owner was then free to focus on bringing in more business and finding other opportunities. More importantly, he was finally able to increase his personal well being and achieved great family dynamics.

There is a great story of a father and son who worked together. The father was a workaholic, but when the son joined him in the business, he told his father, "if you want to work hard then I will play golf, but if you want to play golf, I will work hard." The moral of this story is that sometimes we are so addicted to being the "go to" person that we won't allow even our own child to take responsibility and make important decisions.

Chapter 6

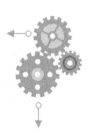

TIME MANAGEMENT:
Why It's Not Just Being on Time

"Tomorrow, Tomorrow, just not today, all lazy men, say"
—**Barry Engel**, translated from a German saying

One of the most common complaints we hear from organizations is that they don't have enough time to accomplish what needs to be done. Another complaint is that people don't show up on time or finish projects on time.

Most people are familiar with time management, but time management is not only about being on time. It's also about working to eliminate time wasters, the things on our to-do list that deceive us into believing that we're being productive. We need to eliminate them completely in order to be more efficient. The more our day controls us, the more we need to control our day.

Stephen Covey says all our time is spent in one of four quadrants, as shown below.

	Urgent	**Not Urgent**
Important	**I** • Crisis • Pressing Issues • Deadlines • Meetings	**II** • Preparation • Planning • Prevention • Relationship building • Personal development
Not Important	**III** • Interruptions • Some mail • Many popular activities	**IV** • Trivia • Some phone calls • Excessive TV/games • Time wasters

Quadrant 1 (Q1) is the quadrant of "Demand," which consists of things that are urgent *and* important. A big client calls, and you need to drop everything. You have to skip lunch because you have a looming deadline. The boss expects everyone to be a meeting he calls. Q1 is full of urgent, in-your-face events, which, if you don't attend, can have serious consequences.

Quadrant 3 (Q3) is the quadrant of "Illusion." Items in this quadrant appear to be important, but they're not. They're merely *urgent*—and usually *someone else's* emergency. To you, they're mostly distractions and interruptions. These deceptive emergencies include a ringing phone, or a new e-mail pop-up, or the buzz of a new text message. These all might contain something important, but most of the time they don't. We have become a society of 24-hour connectedness, but it has come with a huge price. Q3 events steals our concentration and focus. We think that we must reply instantly or else we will be perceived as being out of touch.

Quadrant 4 (Q4) is the quadrant of "Escape," where we do mindless activities because we're so stressed from Q1 and Q3. Unlimited Internet surfing, pointless gaming, checking our messages nonstop, hours on social media, etc., are all symptoms of burnout and stress. The more time we spend in Q1 and Q3, the more we need to escape into Q4. Most people don't realize the price we pay for feeling continuous stress. As an escape we do really stupid and unmitigated things that, at best, are huge wastes of time, and many times unacceptable behavior, just to get away from the feeling of constant pressure.

The answer to overcoming the constant stress and eventual burnout is to spend more time in Quadrant 2 (Q2). It's the quadrant of effectiveness, planning, prevention, relationship-building, and new opportunities. Most of the time, if not all of the time, when projects go wrong it's because we never spent the time needed to plan it properly or thought of ways to prevent problems. Planning and prevention are Q2 activities, because we must act on them; they don't act on us.

The more time you spend in Q2, the less time you will have to spend in the other three. You won't feel so stressed out, and therefore, you wont have the need to escape. You can eliminate Q4 right away, which can save you hours of time. So if you complain about not having enough time, or your boss complains that you're not on time with projects or appointments, check out where and in which quadrants are you spending your time? The most effective people are those in Q1 & 2, not in 3 & 4. It's called living above the line.

Companies are as prone to time wasters as individuals. We never stop to see where our time is being spent. We worked with a real estate title company with a situation that perfectly describes why it's so important to focus on Q2 to be effective in your time management. They were busier than ever, but they were not making more money than in previous years. Their volume was up, but their profits were down. When we analyzed their habits, we realized they were spending most of their time in Q1 and Q3.

They were very busy giving quotes to customers (Q1), gathering all the documents needed for closings but weren't closing at the rates from before (Q3). When we analyzed their closing rate, we found that it had dropped from over 80 percent to under 70 percent, meaning that clients were not following through with their closings and therefore not paying the title company. The title company was putting in a lot of work and not getting compensated. Once we did the analysis, they agreed to meet with their clients that they had a good relationship with and review this problem (Q2). The client that was approached with the data apologized profusely and claimed he just didn't know, and of course, he agreed that the title company needed to get compensated—in other words, Q2 allowed them to identify the problem, correct it, and prevent it from continuing.

Another example is from not-for-profit organization I worked with that was challenged by their unpredictable cash flow. There were certain periods in the year when funds slowed down to a trickle, and they were strapped for cash (Q1). The way they got over the humps was by tapping into their relationships and borrowing large sums of money—short-term of course (Q3). The stress level was very high, and it created huge inefficiencies and cost (Q4). We analyzed the problem and advised them to put together a financial picture that showed their income and expenses and the periodic shortfalls. We had them list all their non-cash holdings, which were substantial, versus their borrowings. We then took this list to a few banks, and they showed interest (Q2). Eventually, the organization received a favorable term sheet that would alleviate the need to run around for borrowed funds (Q3) and instead focus on building their fund-raising capabilities (Q2) and reduce their expenses (Q1).

I recently read an article by Greg McKeown titled "The Unimportance of Practically Everything" in the *Harvard Business Review*:

A friend of mine is the executive director for an organization. He is intelligent and driven, but constantly distracted. At any given time, he will have Twitter, Gmail, Facebook and multiple IM conversations going. The majority of them are useful in some way. Yet, in the back of his mind, he knows there are more important deliverables to get to. But the days slip by and he finds himself working all weekend to catch up. Staying up Sunday night until the early hours of Monday morning has become his modus operandi. It's so bad that he tried having his Executive Assistant pull all of the Internet cables on his computer. But there were still too many ways to get online.

Social media did not create the problem of this man's distraction, but it's clearly an amplifier. Why do otherwise intelligent people find it so easy to get distracted from what really matters?

We live in a world where the majority of things are worthless and few things are exceptionally valuable. Efforts and results are not inherently linked. But this idea is counterintuitive. We assume that if 100 percent of our profits come from 100 percent of our efforts, it stands to reason that any 1 percent of our efforts will result in an equivalent 1 percent of our profits. But this isn't true.

In the late 1700s, Vilfredo Paredo of Italy observed that 80 percent of the land was owned by 20 percent of the people. (This is called the Pareto Principle. We've made a similar observation recently, in that 99 percent of the wealth is owned by 1 percent of the population.) Much later, Joseph Moses Juran, in *The Quality Control Handbook*, applied this principle beyond property ownership, and called it the Law of the Vital Few. The idea, he said, is that if 80 percent of the people have 20 percent of the wealth, then 80 percent of sales come from 20 percent of your customers, 80 percent of profits come from 20 percent of your product line, and so on. Thus, any effort and time focused on that 20 percent will be much more productive than time spent on the other 80 percent. Fix that 20 percent, and you've fixed 80 percent of your problem.

And distinguishing the "vital few" from the "trivial many" can be applied even beyond economics. Sir Isaac Pitman, the inventor of shorthand, discovered that two thirds of the language we use is made up of just 700 words. And according to Nathan Myhrvold, former chief technology officer at Microsoft, "The top software developers are more productive than the average software developers—not by a factor of ten times or one hundred times, or even one thousand times, but by ten thousand." And look at Warren Buffet, who owes 90 percent of his wealth to ten investments. His philosophy is, "You only have to do a few things *right* in your life, so long as you don't do too many things *wrong*."

When it comes to time management, sometimes what you don't do is just as important as what you *do*. Peter Drucker once said to a close friend: "Please do not tell me what you are doing. Tell me what you stopped doing." In other words, we need to look for what is really essential and prioritize it above the non-essentials. We can say no to a thousand projects in our search for the one that is exactly what we're looking for.

Here's a simple idea:

1. Before you leave the office, write down all the most important things you have to do tomorrow on a sticky note.
2. Circle the one that's most important, and leave it on your computer.
3. The next day, accomplish the circled item first thing in the morning. Schedule a window for this project. When you're finished, move on to the rest of that list. If you finish the list, you can branch out and do other things, knowing that you've already done what absolutely has to be done. Also, any time you check e-mail, Twitter, Facebook, and so on, track your distractions. Write down what you did.

The cumulative impact of this small change can be profound.

For those that procrastinate, my father's famously used quote was…

"Morgen, morgen, nur nicht heute, sagen alle faulen Leute"

Loosely translated as, "Tomorrow, Tomorrow, just not today, all lazy men, say"

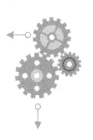

Chapter 7

SMARTPHONES IN THE WORKPLACE:
Are They Really Smart?

How many times have you walked past a table of people eating lunch together, and *every one of them* is texting or e-mailing someone? Although the sight of it always seems somewhat ridiculous, many of us fall prey to the same thing. None of us are innocent. With so much packed into a smartphone, it's no wonder they are a constant attention grabber. And besides, for most people, it's easier to *do* than to *think*.

Surprisingly, and despite the efficiency of having a multifunction communication device at our fingertips, we may not be as productive as we assume we are. Giving half our attention to two places at once may cause us to accomplish much less. This problem is compounded in the workplace. Work needs to get done, and attention needs to be paid to the matter at hand.

The great Peter Drucker, known as the "Father of Modern Management" and grandfather of the modern-day business book, conducted the first large-scale study of a large company (General Motors) more than half a century. Drucker once said, "I never knew a chief executive who could handle more than one priority at a time." Although he said this many years ago, it has never been more pertinent to today's leaders, especially when you consider that we live in the age of distractions.

In addition, the concept of focusing on one thing at a time does not only apply to work. It also applies to personal relationships. Your personal relationships are as important as work, if not more so. And although it is difficult to believe now, there was a time not all that long ago before smartphones and iPads and laptops and e-mails—a time when people had to actually *speak to one another face-to-face*. Work is, of course, an important part of all of our adult lives, but if your relationships don't work, not much will either.

While it is easy to shoot off a text message just to say hi or to check in, you simply cannot build a relationship based on trust with this "shorthand" communication.

Though technology has made communication easier for people who are not in the room with us, it has made it harder for the people who are. We have to draw the line of where our technological communication ends and our human interaction must begin.

Do any of the following scenarios sound familiar to you?

- Workmates or colleagues in a casual exchange around the coffee machine have to repeat themselves as various members drift in and out of the conversation to check their handheld devices.

- Every single person in an update meeting checks his or her phone when a speaker on the conference line is talking.
- A workmate or colleague interrupts an important explanation to show you a picture he has just seen tagged on Facebook.
- Attendees at a seminar reposition themselves near the doorways and halfway out the windows when they realize they can get a signal there.

We've all been there. Very few companies have policies on smartphone use in the workplace, which leaves it up to employees to navigate their way across uncharted waters.

Most people don't intend to be rude. It's just that they aren't mindful about using these indispensable devices in a way that is not offensive to the people around them. Smartphones and manners can be compatible, however, and what follows are a few tips to help raise the bar on phone etiquette.

Give the person in front of you 100 percent of your attention, and don't interrupt a face-to-face conversation by taking a call or texting. Keep your phone stashed in your pocket, handbag, or briefcase when you're attending a business lunch or meeting. People notice you reading under the table more than you think. It's not only distracting and discourteous to the speaker, but also to those around you.

The occasional phone ringing is not as annoying as is scrolling through e-mails, texting, or playing with a new app in your lap. It sends a message to the people in the room that they are not important and that they have lost a battle for your interest against whatever you have going on the screen. If those people are your clients or have power over your job, that's a dangerous message to send.

Yes, sometimes using your phone can be beneficial. You may be able to answer a question instantly with a quick Internet search, or e-mail someone not in the meeting and get a quick answer that you can share with the others present. Or you may want to jot information into your phone that is pertinent to the meeting. There's no hard and fast rule, and that's where using good judgment is important.

But if you're doing something important, the person you're meeting with face-to-face doesn't always know that. All he sees, from his perspective, is you playing with your phone. So if the situation allows, notify him of what you're doing on your phone before you dive in. This is similar to the way that, if you were on the phone with him and had to leave him hanging to take care of something important in person, you would let him know beforehand, instead of just setting the phone down and coming back when he's finished talking.

Sometimes you might be on a deadline for a project and expecting a phone call or e-mail that you must respond to right away. If that's the case, mention it before the meeting begins and then excuse yourself and step away when you take the call. In longer meetings, wait until a break to check e-mails and phone messages.

As a rule, it's smarter to take personal calls in private anyway. Even if you're not sharing highly personal information, it might not be a good idea to have an unwanted audience tuned in to the conversation. Listening to someone talk on a cell phone in a public place is highly amusing; preserve your dignity.

Ironically, the people using smartphones in meetings aren't always lower-level employees. Often they're the managers and leaders. In that case, it can be even more detrimental. After all, leaders set the tone for what's appropriate, and employees tend to follow. Employees interpret leaders using their phone and not paying attention to what's being said as not caring, and if you don't care, why should they? If you're a leader who habitually texts, e-mails, or browses on the phone during meetings, it may be time for some well-deserved introspection. If you can, give the phone to your assistant and ask them to take messages. Another great idea that I heard from one leader was his message that said that he returns phone messages every day after 4 p.m.

In short, when heading to work, it's not necessary to leave your smartphone at home. Whether they are indeed smart or not, they definitely have their merits. Just make sure to use them wisely. Also be aware that using your phone can often be more detrimental than putting it aside, and you have to use your common sense to discern between the two.

Chapter 8

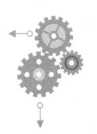

ATTENTION DISORDERS:
The Creative Side of Business

I n people with attention deficit (ADD) and attention deficit hyperactivity
disorder (ADHD), the brain chemicals that regulate attention and brain
activity function differently than in a "normal" person's brain. It's harder
for them to buckle down and concentrate and to anticipate the outcomes of
their actions. On the other hand, it has been recognized that many successful
people have ADD or ADHD. In many cases, it is a critical ingredient to
their success. These people often have an enormous amount of energy and are
highly creative. They tend to be very quick and great thinkers.

Actually, if you are an entrepreneur, you may want to celebrate. People
with ADD/ADHD have made many extraordinary contributions to society,
and it is surprisingly common among high-achieving business founders
and entrepreneurs. Their restless creativity harmonizes well with the high-
drama problem solving associated with running a startup. Here are a few
accomplished businesspeople with ADD/ADHD:

- Richard Branson, founder of Virgin Airlines
- John T. Chambers, CEO of Cisco Systems

- Agathe Christie, author
- Ingvar Kamprad, Swedish founder and chairman of IKEA (He states he adapted the inner workings of his business to compensate for his ADHD and dyslexia.)
- David Needleman, founder and CEO of Jet Blue Airways
- Paul Orfalea, founder and chairperson of Kinko's
- Eleanor Roosevelt, First Lady of the United States of America
- Charles Schwab, founder, chairperson, and CEO of the Charles Schwab Corporation, the largest brokerage firm in the United States

Yet despite these individuals' success, living with ADD/ADHD can be stressful and can cause self-loathing and embarrassment, and it can be a hindrance to productivity. People with ADD/ADHD have trouble focusing on what bores them, can make sloppy errors when rushing (which they frequently do), and have a stronger-than-average tendency to put their foot in their mouth. Their impulsivity can cause them to make unwise or snap decisions, which may run them into quite an expense. Furthermore, they have a tendency to lose patience with those who don't think as quickly as they do and are prone to snap at their employees, thus alienating them.

Alex started his own food business, and it grew quickly—very quickly. Part of his challenge was to hire good people and train them. He found himself taking on more and more responsibilities. His personal coach told him that he had ADD and that he needed to learn how to be patient with his employees, especially the ones who also had ADD/ADHD, and train them well. After reading my articles about delegation, he asked me to come in and train his managers to take on the day-to-day responsibilities so he could focus on growing the company. He actually, for the first time, took a vacation and became comfortable and confident that things are being taken care of. He is now in the process of selling his business and is starting something new (not surprisingly). Alex is just another of the many examples of people with an attention disorder who, when armed with the right tools, can become incredibly successful leaders.

Studies show that of the 5–8 percent of children in the United States with ADHD, 60 percent of them still exhibit those symptoms well into their adulthood. And many of these people live out their entire lives not understanding what makes them different. They internalize the diagnosis of those around them—that they're spacey, careless, reckless, and unreliable—rather than realize the true medical reason behind it all.

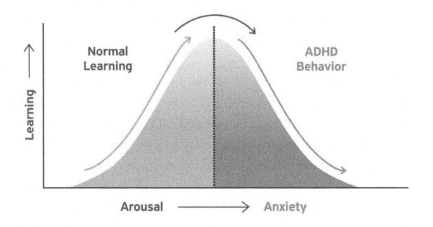

A lot of adults with ADHD live in constant turmoil because of the way their brains function. They have difficulty organizing work, sustaining attention, avoiding distractions, and remembering things. However, under certain circumstances, their brains function quite clearly, which only adds to their confusion.

Furthermore, because of the inconsistency associated with these ADHD impairments, parents, teachers, bosses, and even mental-health professionals experience confusion and may see these contradictory behaviors as flaws. However, brain functions are not something that can be turned on or off at the whim of an individual.

Sometimes medication is needed to help people with attention disorders focus. In the case of Sam, one of my clients, medication helped. When he and his wife came to see me, we devised certain safety plans so Sam didn't make impulsive decisions. We got his wife, a detail-oriented person, more involved in his work. (Note, however, that this does not always work and can sometimes make the relationship even more complicated.) They made a vow to sleep on any big decision. And whenever he started to get frustrated, he would go for a walk or drink a glass of water. Exercise is also known to help the brain slow down. Truly successful business founders with ADD/ADHD are those who have learned to cope when their brains are flooded with information, and their strategies can be helpful for anyone facing information overload.

Managers often have employees who are a challenge to motivate. Consider a scenario where you tell an employee that her performance is not up to par. You take the time to meet with the employee to discuss actions to improve her performance, but no matter what you do, she continues to make the same mistakes. You may form the opinion that she is careless, lazy, or not motivated. However, this assumption may be incorrect. Your employee could simply have ADHD.

Here are a few questions to ask to determine if you or your employee may have ADHD:

- Do you struggle with day-to-day planning, project management, and follow-up?
- Do you lack the systems, discipline, and focus to manage your workload?
- Do you procrastinate too much and fail to accomplish things that need to get done?
- Do you feel you're not as effective and productive as you would like to be?
- Are you easily distracted?

If you answered yes to most of the questions, educate yourself. There are many great books and websites on ADD/ADHD out there. *Driven to Distraction*, *The da Vinci Nation Method*, and *You Mean I'm Not Lazy, Stupid or Crazy?* Are a few good books on the topic. Also, CHADD.org has a list of support groups, self-help tips, and resources.

Many entrepreneurs and business owners with ADD/ADHD get a personal assistant to help them sweat the small stuff. It allows them to free up their minds to brainstorm innovations and solutions. Learn how to harness your unique creativity and positive strengths, and select activities where your traits can have a positive impact on the company. An ADD/ADHD coach can be very helpful in guiding you in the right direction. ADD/ADHD coaches offer techniques geared toward working with the unique brain wiring of individuals with ADD/ADHD.

As a manager, it can be worth your while to try to accommodate your ADHD employee. Adults with attention disorders can bring many positive attributes to the workplace. They can be highly intelligent and creative, and they may also have high energy levels, be very persistent, and take risks. Ideally, those with ADHD will have been diagnosed prior to entering the workforce. But unfortunately, many are not diagnosed until later in life, if at all. Also, because there's a negative stigma attached to ADHD, even a worker who knows he has a disorder may never tell his employer about it and simply just try to do his best without asking for any special accommodations.

But there are accommodations. The following ideas can be useful if you have employees with ADHD, whether or not they've officially been diagnosed as so. As an employer, diagnosing an employee as ADHD on your own can be dangerous as well. But even those who do not have ADHD can have time-management issues.

For example, one major hurdle plaguing those with ADHD is their short attention spans. They're constantly seeking new stimulation and are often distracted. So if the job is sedentary, it may make your employee feel trapped. To benefit her performance, try to assign her work where she can move around. Maybe to be in charge of the office party or some other exciting event, etc. Also try to encourage her to take short breaks throughout the day. Even just getting a cup of coffee or some going to make copies can help her cope better.

Memory can also be a problem for someone with ADD/ADHD. Following up all oral conversations with e-mails, getting your employee to take notes in meetings, and asking him for progress reports frequently will help boost his confidence and efficiency, and will also have a positive effect on all of your organization's employees.

Another idea is to try to block out external distractions. While most people can block out the hum of traffic, the thumping of the copy machine, and the person next to them who has to clear his throat every fifteen seconds, people with ADHD are pulled off their focus by these new stimuli. To minimize external distractions, try to move the employee to a low-traffic area or get him an office with a door he can close.

Sometimes those with ADHD can hyper-focus on one task and miss important engagements, meetings, and even lunch. So it's also important to break tasks into manageable chunks, or set a loud alarm to ring when it's time to break focus.

People with ADHD also have major problems with time management—even worse than the rest of us. They have difficulty organizing their projects and their time, they over-commit and then procrastinate until the last second, and even when they set off on time, a ringing phone or bumping into an old colleague can totally throw them off course and make them late. A good way to keep them focused is to frequently ask them for progress reports.

The main thing is for people with ADD/ADHD to be true to their nature and find a balance in their life—to have fun and make sure they work out, travel, spend quality time with friends and family, and enjoy nature, entertainment, and more. At the same time, they need to employ tools to help them cope with the negative traits associated with ADD/ADHD. After all, people with attention disorders need balance to be able to stay as creative and prosperous as they can be.

PART 3

MAKING IT HAPPEN!

Chapter 9

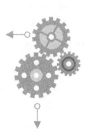

WHAT IS YOUR PURPOSE?
Detecting Your Mission in Life

"We detect, rather than invent, our mission in life."
—Victor Frankl

Habit #9

**Leave this world
a better place than
it was when you got here.**

Mission accomplished.

**Stephen R. Covey
1932-2012**

I find it a sad state of affairs that so many people live out their lives with no particular purpose or aim. Their goal is simply to make it to the end—or even worse, not to bother at all, letting each day come as it may. Some catch onto a fad or two and manage certain aspects of their lives well. Others happily follow a leader along the way. But far too few take responsibility for all aspects of their lives. They don't want to be bothered with having to choose their course and direct the outcomes. (See Introduction).

Viktor Frankl (mentioned in chapter 3) said, "Everyone has his own specific vocation in life. Therein he cannot be replaced, nor can his life be repeated. Thus, everyone's task is as unique as his specific opportunity to implement it. We detect, rather than invent, our mission in life."

Frankl developed a philosophy called Logo therapy, in which an individual can detect his or her unique meaning or mission in life by examining his or her personal vision and values to ensure that they're based on principles and reality. Frankl says that in order to know where we are heading, we need to reexamine the center of our lives. Our center is the source of our security, guidance, wisdom, and power.

After all, what *should* be our center? Centering our lives around people or things outside of ourselves places us at the mercy of uncontrollable changes, mood swings, and inconsistent behavior. So what's the alternative? Being self-centered? This would be too limiting and leads to a lot of unhealthy isolation from others, which can lead to poor mental health.

But by centering our lives on correct principles, on fundamental and classic truths, we create a stable foundation and can then embrace and encompass the truly important areas of our lives. Everything else, successful relationships, professional achievement, and financial security, will then radiate from there. If you take time to define a life course—a mission—and work toward that destination, you will increase the quality of your life. Many times people will, after a life-changing event or mid-life crisis, examine their values and meaning. Leaders in particular need to be clear about their own mission and meaning, as that creates inspired followers. It's also the compass that directs their lives and gives direction to their organization. Without it, they may end up in a direction they never intended.

You might recall this famous passage from *Alice in Wonderland*:

"Would you tell me, please, which way I ought to go from here?"

"That depends a good deal on where you want to get to."

"I don't much care where—"

"Then it doesn't matter which way you go."

Remember the adults in your childhood asking you, "So, what do you want to be when you grow up?" Think about it. Are you, right now, who you wanted to be, what you dreamed you'd be, doing what you always wanted to do? Sometimes people find themselves achieving empty victories and successes at the expense of things that were, at some point, far more valuable to them. "If your ladder is not leaning against the right wall," Covey says, "every step you take gets you to the wrong place faster."

Years ago, I met the CEO of a very large public company who shared with me both his personal mission statement and his observation of why his company was not doing as well. He took a laminated card of his mission statement out of his wallet. The item that made the most impact on me was the line that read "Be Humble." What powerful words. Doesn't that say a tremendous amount about the person, his leadership style, and how he ran his company? He then told me that the greater challenge he was faced with in his company was arrogance. Again, it was a very powerful observation. So having a well thought out personal mission is paramount to knowing in which direction you're planning to travel. You then have a greater chance arriving at your destination.

I remember visiting West Point Academy, and on the wall they proudly displayed their credo, that a cadet "will not lie, steal nor cheat and will not tolerate those that do". I find it to be a very powerful lesson in leadership.

There is something called the mission statement museum, where you can find many mission statements that hopefully will inspire you and others. On the Franklin Covey website there is a mission statement builder that can help you build one.

Our family met a few years ago and over a day of discussion we crafted our family mission statement. It reads:

We are a harmonious family that respects and loves each other by openly communicating, farginning (a Jewish word meaning enjoying other's prosperity), and giving.

We are committed to growing and learning together without **undo pressure** *(these last three words were added by our teenagers!).*

Stephen Covey states that everything is created twice: first as a mental creation, the idea of what your goal is, and second as a physical creation, the actions you take to achieve your goal. We need to get the mental creation right to be able to create and fulfill the physical creation.

Imagine that you're building a house. The first step is to create and refine the blueprints of your dream home. If you don't get the design exactly right first but then decide to change it after you've started building, it will require tremendous time and costly reworking to correct the problems.

To manage others and ourselves effectively we need leadership; in order to lead we need to know what the right thing to do is. We base it on our paradigms and what we feel we want to achieve, but to create a successful, workable, and relevant paradigm we need to figure out what the desired result is. The book *The Secret* discusses the law of attraction, which says that there is power to thoughts; if you think about something, you will attract it to you. It claims that "energy flows where attention goes."

Create what you want in your mind, and your energy will flow in that direction. Knowing what you want (the first creation) will help you recognize everything that is going to support you in achieving what you want (the second creation). You still have to work for it, but the process will be so much more productive, because you will recognize opportunities that will help you.

Visualize your goal clearly. The more detail you have in the representation the better. Make sure you are representing it from the first-person perspective, that is, seeing it through your own eyes. Make it full of vivid colors, hear the sounds, and so on. The better you can experience it, the more powerful it will get.

Create a personal mission statement—a list of values you wish to follow that will help you reach your desired destination. Your circle of influence and level of proactivity will help form these values, as will your roles and responsibilities. Organizations need mission statements. But so do families, so that they do not simply lurch from crisis to crisis and instead know they have principles that will support them. In terms of business, a mission statement can be anything from "Money, money, money" to "Always put the customer first." A friend of mine started a financial services company with a one-word mission statement: "Truth." This, he feels, is what sets his business apart from a lot of the financial services firms out there.

Many companies figure that they can just say something simple, like, "To offer the best service available." But what is the "best service"? Low prices? Excellent customer service? Full money-back guarantee? If you offer everything you can think of, you'll put yourself right out of business.

How Do You Figure Out Your
Professional or Personal Mission Statement?

Like anything else that lasts, writing a mission statement takes time, thought, and creative energy. To come up with a good mission statement, you first have to pose the right questions. If you do, then answering them will help you create a picture of your or your company's mission.

1. **Why are you in your particular business?** What is your goal, as far as yourself, your customers, and your employees? Think about the spark that ignited your interest in starting the business. What will keep this spark burning beyond being just a passing fancy?

2. **What do you sell?** What is the nature of your products or services? What determines pricing? What determines quality? And how does all this relate to the reasons for your business's existence (question #1)? For example, if the reason behind your company's existence is "I can offer good prices", how will all this change when prices go up, or when competitors notice you and start undercutting you?

3. **What level of service do you provide?** Consider, for example, sales, shipping, installation, assembly, customer service, consulting, tech support, and money-back guarantee.

4. **What role is played by you and each of your employees?** Nailing down each person's responsibilities in a way that recognizes their strengths will help you steer your ship.

5. **Who are your customers, and what can you do for them?** How will you make their lives easier, better, or more successful?

6. **When people look at your company, what would you like them to see?** What image do you want to create in the minds of your customers, your suppliers, and the general public?

7. **If you want your customers to boast about your goods and services, what should they say?** How do you differ from your competitors? Most companies believe they offer "the best services available," but do your customers agree? What do you do better, faster, or cheaper?

8. **What kind of relationship will you have with your suppliers?** For example, some suppliers get the feeling that you're only with them for convenience and that you'd drop them the moment something better came along—and they you. Is that what you're going for? Or are you in it together? After all, when one succeeds, so does the other.

9. **How will you use the resources at your disposal to help you reach your goals?** How will you use your capital, technology, products, and services? If you have a strategy, you can focus your energy on your mission, rather than always figuring out what to do next.

10. **What underlying philosophies or values guided your answers to the questions above?** Writing this down helps to clarify the reason behind everything, and sums it up in fewer words. Into one goal, like "Truth."

The Writing Process

Most start-up companies report that the process of putting together a mission statement is often as beneficial as the statement itself. It's like when you're taking notes in school; even if you never read the notes again, the process of writing them down helps you remember and internalize them. The process of writing a mission statement helps clarify your motivations.

- **Set aside several hours to work on your statement.** Writing a mission statement requires a lot of thought and planning, and rushing the process will hinder you from considering everything from all angles. You need to come up with a statement that simultaneously sums up everything the business is and inspires what the business will become. You can't rush creativity. Set aside a specific date and time, and find a quiet place with no interruptions.

- **Involve other people.** Don't do this yourself. Get your employees in on the process. If you're a sole proprietor, consider including close friends, supportive family members, or even your accountant. Getting more heads involved will help you come up with ideas, spot flaws you'd otherwise miss, and provide the encouragement you need if it gets to be too much. As important, it will help you to secure buy-in when you need it most. "Lone rangers," or "cowboys," often find themselves alone when they need their colleagues the most (regardless of where that long ranger sits on the organizational chart).

- **Come prepared.** Not everyone knows what a mission statement is or what you have in mind, so be prepared to explain to everyone involved what it is you're doing. You also might want to provide pens, paper, company background information, and refreshments. If everyone is involved, everyone will feel attached and committed to the statement later.

- **Brainstorm**. Look at sample mission statements for inspiration, and then try to come up with your own answers to the questions above. Write down every idea anyone comes up with, even if it sounds silly. There is no bad idea in a brainstorm. Harping on what does and doesn't work in each individual plan grinds the creative part of the session to a halt, and it's difficult to get it started again. You can always discuss and weed out the silly ideas later.

- **Put together the best parts.** Have everyone write down what they think were the best ideas of the brainstorming session, and then put all the statements together. Polish up the language, and add lots of active words that create dynamic, visual images that paint clear mental images and inspire action.

Once your statement is complete, get it out there. Hang it around the office, use it in your email signature, and put it on your brochures, business plans, and business cards. Everyone—inside and outside the business—needs to see it, internalize it, and know that you know where you're going.

Chapter 10

USE SMART GOALS
IN WISE PLANNING

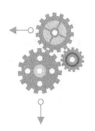

Specific

Measurable

~~**A**ttainable~~ **A**mbitious

Relevant

Timed

T he purpose of goals is not to help us achieve mediocre results, but to help us achieve extraordinary results. The term *strategic planning* has become very popular in recent years. One of my favorite curiosity exercises is to look back through history to learn where certain terms and concepts came from. Before the 1960s and Peter Drucker, the term "strategy" was used as a solely military term. Put another way, half-a-century ago, no one had ever used the word "strategy" and "business" together. When Drucker approached publishers in the 1960s with the term "management strategy," he was rebuffed. His publisher explained that no one would understand the use of a military term like "strategy" in a business context. The corporate world did not accept the term "strategic management," (and in turn, strategic planning), until more than a decade later.

Today, of course the world has progressed quite a distance from where it was then. Many businesses and organizations now talk about doing strategic planning, as it provides a basis for monitoring progress and for assessing results and impact. It facilitates development and enables an organization or business to look into the future in an orderly and systematic way.

In strategic planning, a leader develops a vision for the organization's future, focusing on long-term goals rather than short-term objectives. He or she then determines the necessary priorities and procedures to achieve that vision, breaking it down into measurable, realistic units.

Strategic planning is an ongoing process of self-examination, confrontation of difficult choices, and establishment of priorities. It involves charting a course that you believe is wise, and adjusting that course as you gain more information and experience.

Strategic planning is defined as the process of addressing the following questions:

- Where are we?
- What do we have to work with?
- Where do we want to be?
- How do we get there?

The first step is to address the questions "Where are we?" and "What do we have to work with?" Your answer to the first question defines your current company and gives you your starting point. Answering the second question involves a consideration of strengths and weaknesses and a determination of how to capitalize on strengths.

The next step in the process is answering, "Where do we want to be?" As the articulated vision stems from the values of those involved in the process, it is essential that this step involve everyone who will have a stake in achieving the vision. The vision is then translated into a mission statement: a broad, comprehensive statement of the purpose of the company or business. (You will recall the steps for crafting a mission statement from the previous chapter.)

Once you determine your goals, you need to decide how to reach them. This step involves articulating strategies that recognize the strengths and weaknesses of the business and how to use them to achieve a goal.

Many organizations are familiar with the SMART acrynom for goal setting: specific, measurable, attainable, relevant, and time-bound. These are great tools in helping us accomplish our goals. Paul J. Meyer describes the characteristics of SMART goals in *Attitude Is Everything*.

In our strategic planning work with companies, we start by asking all participants what are the their five top goals they want to achieve, both personal and professional. We then want them to create their plan using the SMART criterea. However, to produce extraordinary results, we need to look specifically at BAG's: *Big Ambitious Goals*.

One of the questions I suggest asking new hirees is, what is your five-year goal? Where do you want to be, and why? It shows a lot about their determination and ambition. Some people are afraid of hiring people who say they want to own their own business. My argument for hiring these people is that they will be very motivated to succeed and help the organization to grow.

Specific

While general goals are easy to come up with, they are often too vague and don't really tell anyone what actions are expected of them. But if the goals are specific, they are clear and unambiguous, and they tell everyone exactly what is involved so that they can figure out what to do first, and who should be doing it.

A good, specific goal answers the five *W Questions*:

- **What:** What do we want to accomplish?
- **Why:** For what reasons are we doing this? What would be the benefits of reaching our goal?
- **Who:** Who would be involved?
- **Where:** What location?
- **Which:** What are the requirements and constraints involved?

Measurable

Unless there are some concrete criteria for measuring when a goal is achieved or how close you are to achieving it, it's impossible to know whether your team is making progress at any given point. If you can measure progress, you can make sure you're on track and reach target dates for specific steps of the goal, and experience the exhilaration of reaching those mini-goals that will spur you on to reach the ultimate goal.

A measurable goal will answer the following questions:

- How many? (Steps, mini-goals, units of achievement, etc.)
- How much? (Effort, progress by a certain date, etc.)
- How will we know when we've hit our goals?

Ambitious

All goals need to be realistic and attainable, or you're setting yourself up for disappointment. An attainable goal may be challenging and difficult to reach, and beyond everyone's comfort zone, but it's not impossible. Nor can it be too simple to reach, or it will be meaningless.

An attainable goal will usually answer this question:

- **How:** How can the goal be accomplished?

An *ambitious* goal, in the meantime, will ask:

- What *else* can we accomplish? What would happen if we *really* stretch? Can we accomplish *more*?

Relevant

Any goal, to be worth this kind of time and effort, has to *matter*. An office manager's goal to "Mow sixteen lawns by 5 p.m." may be specific, measurable, attainable, ambitious, and time-bound, but it's not relevant. Many of your goals will need support from your boss, your boss's boss, and the members of your team. Only relevant goals will receive that support; a goal that is relevant drives the grand plan of the company forward, and will receive the support of everyone in that company.

A relevant goal answers the following questions (with the correct answer always being yes):

- Is this worthwhile?
- Is this the right time?
- Are you the right person/people to do this?
- Does this match our efforts and needs?

Time-Bound

Did you start your diet today? It's definitely on your to-do list. But it's not until we have a wedding coming up that we actually start starving ourselves. Giving ourselves a target date helps us stay focused and not stray from the path when other emergencies come up. Having a time-bound goal helps establish a sense of urgency.

A time-bound goal will usually answer the questions:

- By when do we need to be finished?
- What do we need to have done six months from now?
- What do we need to have done six *weeks* from now?
- What do we need to do *today*?

Here is an example of how using strategic planning helped achieve a SMART BAG. Sam had many challenges getting a line of credit from a bank.

His company had a poor credit rating and negative equity on its balance sheet. Sam shared with me that his goal was to get the banks to help fund some of the cash-flow needs.

I asked Sam, "If you could get the banks to give you whatever you need, what do you really need?" He said "Two million dollars: one million to buy the building I'm in and the other for new machinery, additional inventory, and improved cash flow."

Now we had a Big Ambitious Goal: two million dollars in two years.

I told Sam it would take him two years to achieve those goals, but he needed to stick with the plan I made for him. He agreed, and we put together the SMART BAG plan. We followed the plan carefully, and I introduced him to a banker I was friendly with. We had a very specific strategy for getting the bank to want to offer him a line of credit.

At the end of six months, he was able to get $250,000 for his cash-flow needs. We then invited in the first bank and as well as a second bank to look at the possibility of financing the purchase of the building. It ended up that both banks wanted the business, so now we had competition and were able to negotiate a great deal for Sam. Two years later he owned the building.

There are many approaches to strategic planning and different models available to implement them. There is no one perfect strategic-planning model for each business. It depends on what your business needs. For example, if planning is meant to add a new product or program, the process will probably include market research to verify the need, markets, pricing, and so on for the new product or service.

The strategy depends on whether the business has done planning before. For example, if the organization has not, extensive attention to mission, vision, and values statements is probably warranted. It also depends on whether the environment of the business or organization is changing rapidly and whether the business has had past success in planning.

Each organization ends up developing its own nature and model of strategic planning, often by selecting a model and modifying it as it goes along in developing its own planning process.

You can follow this very basic outline:

1. Identify your purpose. This is the statement that describes why your organization exists. Define or review your organization's values. Be sure there is a consensus on why your business or organization exists, what goals or outcomes it seeks to achieve, what it stands for, and whom it serves.

2. Establish a vision statement. This statement describes the future state of your customers/clients and your business at some point in the future.

3. Select the goals your organization must reach if it is to work effectively toward your mission and achieve your vision. The SMART BAG is a great place to start. Identify specific approaches and strategies that must be implemented to reach each goal.

4. Compile the mission, vision, strategy, and action plans into a strategic-plan document, where you finalize a summary of the results and decisions of the strategic planning process. There doesn't have to be a set format, but be sure to include the outputs of each major step. Ensure that upper management approves the plan.

5. Monitor implementation of the plan, and update the plan as needed. Build in procedures for monitoring and for modifying strategies based on changes in the business.

Whatever model you'll be implementing, the key planning sessions often work best when facilitated by an outsider who is knowledgeable about the business or about businesses and organizations in general. A facilitator should be someone skilled in-group processes and experienced in strategic planning. They should be nondirective, committed to ensuring full discussion of issues, but also task-oriented and able to move the process forward. We used a facilitator when we formulated our personal family mission statement; they helped us keep focused and allowed family members to freely express their thoughts.

Sometimes a former board member or executive director can fulfill this role in a business sense. For family mission statements, a close outside relative, friend, or community or spiritual leader can be a facilitator. Agreeing on values, vision, and mission is usually best accomplished as a part of a planning retreat or at a special meeting.

In your business, there must be someone within the organization who can take responsibility for implementing the strategy. Be sure progress toward goals and objectives and the use of strategies is monitored regularly. Strategies should be revised and annual objectives developed based on the progress made, the obstacles encountered, and the changing environment. The board plays a critical role in reviewing progress and ensuring that strategies are changed as appropriate.

Specific criteria for evaluating and choosing among strategies should be agreed on. In doing this, the planning group should always consider the need to clearly define responsibilities for their implementation.

Many organizations are very focused on short-term goals, and some even focus on long-term goals. But to achieve extraordinary results, you need to aim for the stars, because if you aim for the stars, you at least land on the moon. Don't be afraid to plan big. But to do so, you need to have a strategic plan and the handy SMART tools to make it happen!

Chapter 11

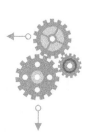

CRITICAL THINKING:
Criticizing Is Not Thinking

G ood thinking skills are essential for making good decisions. Good decisions require critical thinking, be they personal decisions, vocational decisions, or civic decisions. The term *critical thinking* refers to the many ways we can think through an issue to come to a conclusion, as opposed to just picking a one-sided route and following it through to the end.

Although the word *critical* is sometimes used in a negative sense, *critical thinking* is actually very positive. Like other dispositions and abilities, critical thinking can be learned and improved if we work at it. It is worth learning to think critically, because the personal benefits are many; we need to make the best possible decisions in order to survive in this difficult world. A critical thinker is also someone with the vision to see around the corner and plan for the unexpected.

Wayne Gretzky was a world-renowned hockey player. He was once asked what his secret to greatness was. Did he skate quicker, better, or faster? None of the above, he answered. He "just figures out where the puck is going next and gets there first."

What is a critical thinker?

A critical thinker has seven basic traits:

1. Someone who is open minded and sees that any given way is not the *only* way.
2. Someone who is well informed, or at least well informed enough to know when he isn't.
3. Someone who can put together relevant information from various sources and interprets it effectively.
4. Someone who can tell which sources are actually relevant and which of those are reliable.
5. Someone who can then draw logical assumptions and conclusions.
6. Someone who raises important problems and formulates them clearly (as opposed to making blank statements, like, "Nah, I don't like it").
7. Someone who can defend her position or conclusion through clear, logical reasoning.

Critical thinkers do not let emotion get the better of them. They are not attached to any one suggestion because they were the one who came up with it, nor do they shoot down a decision because the person who came up with it is the most annoying guy in the office. They are open-minded and can evaluate and criticize their own thinking as well as they can anyone else's. They are not married to their own ideas.

More than just an emotional state of mind, critical thinking allows us to approach a problem in new and creative ways, as opposed to assuming that the topic at hand falls into a pre-determined category of problems with a set solution. Not every problem can be tackled in the same way that something that has in the past. If you approach the problem critically, you may be able to offer multiple solutions to the same problem in new and inventive ways. In addition, critically pulling apart the roots of an idea can inspire new ideas for other situations. Figuring out how to deal with large orders, for example, may help optimize the fulfillment process for even small orders.

On top of that, critical thinking forces a team to look at a situation and weigh all the possible solutions before coming up with a final answer. Everyone's input is important, as contribution from many people diminishes the possibility that any issues will be overlooked, and it increases the likelihood of the team coming up with a good solution. It also encourages teamwork and gives each employee the chance to contribute to the future of the organization, so they don't feel like they're solely working to further someone else's ideas.

And in fact, the Department of Labor has identified critical thinking as the raw material that underlies a competent workplace, as far as problem solving, planning, and risk management. It's also been rated the number-one skill of increasing importance over the next five years, according to a national survey of employers.

Yet one of the biggest hurdles for managers is the lack of critical-thinking abilities of people in their organizations. So how do you measure and increase it? Dr. Edward De Bono is considered one of the great critical thinkers of our time and has written many books on the subject. One of our seminars was based on his book called *The Six Hats of Critical Thinking*. De Bono suggests there are six ways to think and that we can move through all of them and still reach a conclusion in a harmonious and efficient way.

If you've ever been in a business meeting, you may have come to the conclusion that they are a horrendous waste of time. In many cases, most of meetings are spent arguing points back and forth, with each person continuously repeating himself until it's time to go home. The owner of an idea enthusiastically promotes it, despite any flaws, because it was her idea. Others try and knock it down because all they see are the flaws. And then you have the skeptics, who don't like *anything*, and the optimists, who are going to see the positive side of every idea, even if it runs counter to the entire business plan, or they're simply afraid of disagreeing with the boss. People talk *at* each other instead of *with* each other, and people don't really listen to what anyone else has to say as much as they just wait for their turn to speak.

De Bono has a great approach that is simple yet brilliant. It's called the Six Thinking Hats. In this system, each way of thinking is represented by a different color hat: The white hat represents factual thinking, and the red hat represents emotional thinking. Creative thinking is represented by the green hat, process thinking by blue, optimism by yellow, and pessimism by black.

The Six Thinking hats can help in the following examples: The CEO of a company announced that he'd like to buy another company. The controller was concerned with the funding and how it would affect the bottom line, and the managers were concerned about how it would affect their departments. Each person represented only his own perspective. Or the situation can be flipped: A manager can be trying to sell her boss a new idea, and the boss continuously shoots it down, so the manager eventually becomes gun shy about expressing new ideas. All these people can be making valid points, but the problem is that each side gets frustrated because people aren't seeing their point of view.

Dr. Edward De Bono's
Six Thinking Hats

White Hat
Information Available &
Needed, Facts, Data

Red Hat
Intuition, Hunches,
Feelings, Emotion

Yellow Hat
Benefits, Value,
Positive Aspects

Black Hat
Caution, Difficulties,
Risks, Weaknesses

Green Hat
Creative Ideas,
Alternatives, Possibilities

Blue Hat
Managing the Thinking,
Focus, Summary

Here is how the Six Thinking Hats method works:

The boss or facilitator starts a meeting by putting on (literally or conceptually) the white hat, which represents all the relevant facts, numbers, and background information that he and the members of the team know, with no emotions, projections, or speculations—nothing that isn't 100 percent factual. No disputing is allowed at this point. In other words, instead of making an emotional decision and then getting the facts, get the facts first, and then bring in the emotions. The manager at this stage also presents his idea.

At that point, he puts on the red hat, which means that all the team members write down, in a couple of words, their gut emotional reaction to the new idea. Red represents emotions, which come from the heart. No explanations or apologies are necessary.

Once that is out of the way, he puts on the yellow hat, and everyone writes down all of the positive, sunny, optimistic things about the idea, and everyone compares notes. The natural optimist may have a long list, while the natural pessimist may have a short one.

When everyone is finished, the facilitator put on his black hat, and everyone writes down pessimistic thoughts—the reasons this idea might not work or might not be the best idea, or would take resources away from the company's ultimate goals. Note that the black-hat thinkers are not actually negative, but cautious thinkers who safeguard against ideas that might destroy the company. So with the Six Thinking Hats method, this becomes clear and removes the possibility of any offense.

After everyone has come up with reasons that the idea might not work, the facilitator puts on the green hat, which represents growth and creativity. Everyone tries to think of creative solutions to the problems expressed by the black hat or alternatives to the original idea in light of the issues expressed by the black hat.

In addition, throughout the meeting, the process is steered at several times by the blue hat, which represents process thinking, or the flow of action, like water, from how the meeting will be structured, to the order of the hats, to what steps will be taken to put the plan into action once it's decided.

Once the team has gone through all the hats, the discussion should be simple and the decision more well rounded, without egos involved. It allows all the points to be discussed without each person feeling that his thoughts were shut down or ignored, and it teaches people to think creatively and to see an issue from another person's point of view. And because everyone is focused on a particular approach at any one time, the group tends to be more collaborative.

On a personal level, people can look at some or all of the thinking points and ask themselves the same questions. In the above mentioned Jewish ethics book, *Duties of the Heart (Mind)*, written over a thousand years ago, the author goes through a very similar process in detail, about whether he should write his book or not. It is fascinating to read the thought process he employed, in which he examines all the pros and cons, including what others might think or say.

This process can furthermore be used in any business decision, including asking customers about your product—what they liked, what they didn't like, what they think you can do better, whether it met their needs, and so on. For example, after the training, the De Bono Company asked me to rate their seminar, using the Six Thinking Hats process. They asked me what I thought was positive (I thought that the process helped our participants make better decisions) and what was negative (some of the attendees felt the presentation could use more opportunities for audience participation). The structure of this process allowed me to be open and honest about what worked and what didn't work, without worrying about hurt feelings. After all, they *asked* me to say something negative.

Thinking things through on all six levels gives clarity and the chance for everyone to express their thoughts and emotions in a safe and positive environment. Try it! You might like it, and you might not care that you're called a black hat.

Chapter 12

Delegation and Teamwork:
The Keys to Leadership

"Inspect what you Expect"
—W. Edwards Deming

I f you want something done right, you have to do it yourself. Or so they say. Here are two of the most common complaints we hear from business and organization leaders:

1. "It's so difficult to find people who are willing to take responsibility," and
2. "It's so hard to train people in all the little details; I'd rather just do the work myself."

Meanwhile, here are the most common complaints we hear from employees:

1. "My boss doesn't trust me to make any decisions," and
2. "I have no authority, but I get blamed for everything that goes wrong."

91

So why is it that the perspectives of leaders and their employees are so far apart? Many of the organizations that I'm asked to evaluate ask why there is so much stress and managers or executives feel close to burnout. The answer is mostly because there is little delegation and teamwork, if any.

Delegation requires the upfront work of defining each and everyone's responsibilities and creating a win-win agreement. Many times, agreements are one sided and are either good for the employers or good for the employees. Neither will work out over time. Delegating responsibilities is not the same as delegating jobs. Responsibilities are defined by what are you responsible for, the results or outcome that we expect. Jobs are tasks that people will ask you to do but it doesn't describe the outcome or results. Leaders needs to be clear about what the responsibilities are that they expect from their people and how they will be held accountable. Remember to "*Inspect what you Expect.*"

The secret to great teamwork is allowing the team to take on responsibilities and have authority to make good decisions. Some organizations promote the idea of a "champion" (i.e., a person or persons who take on a project and champion it). Some create team leaders with the same intent. The principle of these kinds of ideas is to allow people to step up to the plate and get the recognition for success. Leaders, however, need to be very careful not to "dump" a project on a person and not to tie a person's hands behind their back. This means that effective leaders must delegate important and visible projects, ones where team members can get recognition, and allow them to make decisions based upon agreed-upon guidelines. A method that I use successfully is to agree that the team leaders or champions need to discuss their recommendations with the leadership, and the leadership needs to respond within a given time, say 24–48 hours, otherwise the team leader can go ahead. This gives the team the responsibility to make good recommendations yet doesn't allow the leadership to create bottlenecks.

So how do we empower our people to take on responsibilities, and how do we give them the proper authority? The way to do it is to create upfront a true win-win agreement. The way to create a win-win agreement is to use what Stephen Covey calls "Dr. Grac."

The Dr. Grac acronym lists a series of ideas that, if discussed up front, cover all the bases so that the boss is confident leaving the job in the employees' hands, and the employees are confident accepting the responsibility.

- **Desired Results**: explaining the responsibility of the job or task as well as the outcomes that are expected
- **Guidelines**: agreeing to the rules of what can and can't be done
- **Resources**: discussing what resources are available to the employee to help him complete the task, such as financial resources, research materials, people, and tools
- **Accountability**: agreeing on how the boss will inspect the work and how it will be evaluated
- **Consequences**: what the employee can expect to happen if the project meets expectations and what will happen if it doesn't

Here is an example of how we helped a company apply the Dr. Grac system effectively. Joel hired Mike to be the bookkeeper of his company and really wanted Mike to take over the responsibility of, as Joel put it, "tracking all the financials." However, Joel didn't explain in detail what that meant. Mike wasn't sure how he should go about taking the responsibility of the financials, where his job started and ended, or what kinds of questions he was expected to ask as opposed to which questions could cost him his job. While both had a great work ethic, they weren't accomplishing as much as they could have. When we sat down with them, we advised Joel to use the Dr. Grac model.

Desired Results: At the point that we met with Joel, the financials were held in different projects by different people, as opposed to being shared by the company as a whole. The challenge was that each employee was operating in his own "silo" and didn't really know or understand what was going on in other departments. They didn't understand the company-wide cash flow needs, the accountants' requirements, how to build a line of credit, and so on. We wanted to bring all the financials under one roof and made Mike responsible for having the various numbers available in a timely manner. He would have the cash-flow requirements and projections for Joel on a daily basis (so he could easily see which entity had a surplus, for example) and prepare the reports for the accountants (so Joel didn't have to pay double for their work as well), which would also be used as a report for the banks, so that Joel could build credit with them.

Guidelines: To accomplish the above, we had each of the owners explain to Mike what he was currently doing, and Mike would develop a plan for each person to make sure he was getting the numbers in a timely manner and in the format that he needed it with the proper backup.

Resources: We advised Mike to have an up-to-date accounting and management system to track all the numbers. Joel gave him access to all the data and any additional training he needed (Excel, accounting software, and so on). Mike then had access to their accountants, their consultants, and any outside help he needed.

Accountability: Mike then would report to the owner, who reviewed all the financials on a monthly basis and made sure that everyone was reporting accordingly and helping Mike get the process up and running smoothly. Joel would also have the departments be subject to Mike's reviews (on top of each of them being subject to their respective managers' reviews) and gave Mike the authority to make necessary changes, with Joel's approval.

Consequences: We believed that this project would take six to twelve months, over the course of which Joel expected Mike to have total responsibility and authority. After that period, Joel decided to promote Mike to controller and increase his pay accordingly. Joel also began looking to get a line of credit from the banks for future growth, and Mike would receive an extra bonus for that.

By taking the time to explain, plan, and train, employers and their employees can agree to the outcomes and expectations. Otherwise each assumes that they understand what the job is all about, even though those assumptions might not line up.

Here is how you can apply the Dr. Grac system to your own organization. First, create an organizational chart that outlines the different responsibilities like financials, sales and marketing, manufacturing, distribution, purchasing, and so on. Then fill in the names of the people currently holding those jobs, and write down what they are responsible for and to whom they report. If you find that you have responsibilities with no names attached, then those are the areas that you need to fill.

Once that's done, meet with your teams and share the org chart. Explain what you've done, and make sure everyone understands and agrees on their responsibilities and reporting structure. Then meet with your managers individually and create a win-win agreement. Remember, it needs to be good for both sides; you need to feel that they are taking responsibility and willing to be held accountable for the results, and they need to feel that they have the proper resources and guidelines to accomplish the job. You will need to hold their hand for a short while, offering encouragement maybe even coaching, with the aim of having them feel responsible and accountable. Eventually, however, they will feel empowered and confident to be fully responsible and accountable. Once you've accomplished this step with all your managers, you have basically pushed all of your day-to-day responsibilities down to the next level and now have the time and headspace to focus on the future or more exciting things. Remember, the most successful managers are those that manage themselves out of a job!

According to many management experts, your focus before the project or job begins should or could be the following six questions:

1. **Who** is responsible, and who else is involved?
2. **What** are the goals and results you are looking for?
3. **When** (or *by* when) do you need to see results?
4. **Where** is the job taking place? (For example, 50 percent travel required, or the job is being done from home.)
5. **Why** is the job important?
6. **How** you going to achieve the results?

Another important reason to use one or both of the methods above is because many companies operate in silos or fiefdoms (mini companies), meaning that the departments and people do not cooperate or collaborate with each other. Every man is an island. That was exactly the type of organization that Jack Welch found when he became Chairman and CEO of General Electric (at age 44) in 1981. GE was known as "the C-word." A conglomerate—or a bunch of companies that had little to do with each other. Welch hated the fact that his company was called a conglomerate. Even worse is what Welch found *inside* many of the companies that were now under his leadership.

You guessed it—silos and fiefdoms galore—companies in which the marketing department never talked to manufacturing, and manufacturing department heads never talked to the sales people. To him, that was the essence of bureaucracy, and bureaucracy is the enemy of productivity. Welch spent the next two decades reinventing GE, "blowing up the bureaucracy," and taking down the walls that he was sure were killing his businesses. He called this new model "boundary less" companies, and he made sure that all of the businesses were either #1 or #2 in each of their industries they competed within; if they were not market leaders, those businesses got "fixed, closed, or sold." (He got #1 and #2 from Peter Drucker, with whom Welch met secretly a few weeks before becoming CEO in the spring of 1981). But the newly appointed CEO knew that he could achieve nothing if he did not spend years fixing the culture, making sure that all of his 200,000+ employees worked together as a cohesive company in which everyone "read from the same sheet of music." In all the years he led GE, Jack Welch never stopped talking about all of the ills associated with a bloated bureaucracy and always felt he could do more to streamline the organization and rid the company of red tape.

The problem with a bureaucratic culture is that when problems arise, and they always do, there is nothing but finger pointing. People blame everybody else and never take responsibility for their own actions. That is why great managers like Jack Welch fought so hard against fiefdoms and the hurtful mentality that proliferated in these poisonous organizations. While he did believe in giving anyone who lived the values of the organization a second chance, his "gut" instinct was to fire "bully-like" managers who screamed and undermined his employees when things went wrong. Welch had zero patience for conflict that was brought on by anyone in the organization.

When an organization has a serious amount of inner-*conflict*, it fails. When it has *compliance* and *communication*, it succeeds. But when is has *cooperation* and *collaboration*, it prospers. That is what Welch's boundary less businesses were all about—people working together all bound by a common set of values and ethics. Cooperation and collaboration should be the cost of admission in any well-run organization. Ultimately, you as a manager are responsible for creating your team and their teamwork. That's your Dr. Grac. So if there's no team or teamwork, you haven't done your part and need to hold yourself accountable before holding your employees responsible.

Chapter 13

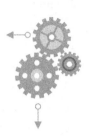

KNOW YOUR MANAGEMENT STYLE:
Overcome Dysfunctional Leadership

"Work more on your business than in your business"
—Michael Gerber

R oy Cammarano, (See forward) in his very insightful book *Entrepreneurial Transitions: From Entrepreneurial Genius to Visionary Leader,* has studied hundreds, if not thousands, of managers and leaders, especially entrepreneurs. In his seminars and training, he explains how most managers are either very hands-on or very hands-off, or they start off as one and then become the other.

Understanding one's management style allows the leader to step back and see what's working and what's not. Too often it's the leadership that stifles their employees or is too laid back, and they don't recognize what they are doing wrong. Roy has trained me in his methodology (I'm the only one so far that he has trained and allows to use his methods), and it's very interesting for me to see how most managers and leaders fall into one of the two categories of either being hands on or hands off. Another very important evaluation is what Roy calls The 6'Cs. Basically, organizations that have internal conflict and competition will fail. Those that can attain internal compliance and communication succeed. And those that internally cooperate and collaborate will prosper. (See diagram in the Foreword). When organizations tend to finger point and blame shift, its apparent they are in the conflict and competition stage. Unless the leadership gets their act together, quickly, there may be dire ramifications including failure of the business. Many times it's the very good people that leave and the mediocre stay on. Sometimes it's that people are just giving much less of themselves because of the conflicts. In the compliance and communication stage, things will be directed from the top and clearly communicated. Organizations can be successful, however, the innovation and inspiration will be gone. People will feel like they are robots and their opinions don't count much. As one person quipped, "if you're paying me to come, you might as well get my brains too". The very good people will eventually be frustrated enough to leave, to be replaced by someone that doesn't mind (yet) to be a gofer (go for this and go for that). For *prosperity* to flourish there needs to be collaboration and cooperation. A good way to understand the difference between the two, is, if I cooperate with you then I will explain how things are done, if I collaborate the I will do it so you can see how its done. Let me give you an example. I was once in Montreal and while checking in, the receptionist asked my wife and I if we need a Wi-Fi connection. She then asked us if we would like her to update the phones and when it's done, she would return it to us. That is being collaborative.

When Roy flew in to do a training seminar, we invited a group of entrepreneurs and managers, and each confirmed how true and accurate his analysis was. One of the participants was Jack, who had previously been a highly successful lawyer and then decided to start his own real estate firm. He was able to get serious financial backing for acquiring and renovating multi family apartments. He started acquiring buildings and hiring staff at a very quick pace. But he was working harder and longer hours to keep pace. Sometimes he was still awake at three in the morning e-mailing his managers, telling them what to do the next day. He controlled every aspect of the business. Nothing happened without him making the decision or giving his consent.

Then he attended the seminar by Roy and, in his own words, "it was transformational." He realized that that he was "headed for a heart attack" if he didn't change how he managed his people and processes. Rather than wanting to control every decision himself, he needed to allow others to take on responsibility and provide them with the necessary guidance. He then started hiring people who could take full responsibility, and he started giving them authority. Every process was well defined *before* the job, not during. He started focusing on what he did best and what was important for the company. His life changed, and so did his business. The first step was to create a "process room" where every department listed exactly each step of the process. For example, there was a clear, written out, step-by-step list of functions such as, acquisition, renovation, finding renters, maintenance, and so on. They also defined who was responsible and accountable. While it took months to get it all up on the wall, it allowed people to understand what their job responsibility was, and it clarified expectations. Weekly management meetings were an important part of the process, and they allowed people to share with each other and be updated.

Jack is an example of what Roy calls the Entrepreneurial Genius. This first level is when a person starts their own business or organization from scratch and is the genius behind the idea. They are involved in every aspect and usually it's a one-man show until they can afford to hire other people to help out. Things usually go well as long as the owner has good business smarts and understand the process.

But at the next level we usually find the hands-on-everything, make-every-decision type of leader, which Roy calls the Benevolent Dictator (BD). These types of leaders become the "fatherly" figure and are involved in every aspect of the running the organization. Everything must flow through them, and they feel they are the only one capable of making all the decisions. So they "dictate" instead of participate, as they believe that other people are just not capable of making good decisions.

The problem with the BD is that nobody likes to work for a dictator, even a benevolent one, as it makes them feel like robots or gofers without any input or say. Employees feel worthless and are subject to the whims and fancies of the irrational thinking and decisions of the BD. Because the BD doesn't ask for input, they are clueless to the fact that their employees are very unhappy and only stay because they can't find another job. It is almost as though the BD can hire only those who have no mind of their own, or as though they are asked to leave their brains at the door. The BD might say something like, "In this company we ask you to 'do,' not 'think.'"

However, the dictator eventually and inevitably becomes so stressed out because she believes that the only way the business or organization can be successful is if she controls the people. So she becomes a control freak. That then takes a toll on her; she suffers either emotionally, or physically, or both. Of course, she blames everyone but herself. If everyone would just listen to her, everything would be perfect—or so she thinks.

When she tries to ease up or is forced by her employees to give up some authority, she usually goes to the other extreme. Cammarano calls this the Disassociated Director (DD), which is the "hands-off" type of a leader. She typically allows everyone to do as they please, has little or no oversight or accountability, and allows them to create their own fiefdoms and silos and that creates even bigger problems.

Employees start to act on their own and some even become mini dictators, and over time they begin to believe that they are running their own little business. They resist cooperation, so collaboration suffers. And they hate it when the boss tries to wiggle back in and make decisions. They become protective of their turf, and turf wars start to happen. Finger pointing and blame is the most common outcome, and that's when the business starts to suffer. When there is conflict and competition, there will be failure.

Sometimes, as a last measure, the boss decides to jump back in, but it is usually way too late. The employees have become entrenched, and they control the day-to-day operations and the culture of the company. This animosity causes people to leave when push comes to shove, and they usually take parts of the business with them. The boss then starts to wonder what he is doing there and what his job is. He resents the fact that nobody really needs or wants his input and decisions. He may create a crisis so he can jump back in and extinguish it. He thinks this will prove his mettle and his importance. But his people see through it and highly resent it, which takes a toll on the company. It becomes a vicious cycle.

Anyone working for one of these two dysfunctional manager types can tell you that these descriptions are very accurate. The last thing that you, as a leader, want is to become either of these types. Yet we all lean one-way or the other. Here are some questions you can ask yourself to determine your management style.

1. Do I need everyone to ask me exactly what needs to be done?
2. Do I tell people what to do on a constant basis?
3. Do I look over their shoulders and their computer screens?
4. Am I constantly short tempered and impatient with my people?
5. Do I believe that most employees are just plain lazy or incompetent or both?
6. Do I get upset and stressed out because people are always "messing up"?
7. Am I always blaming everyone else for mistakes?
8. Do I feel as if the events are controlling me and I'm not in control of the events?
9. Do I resent not being asked to make every decision?
10. Do I feel like my people would rather I don't come into the office?

If you answered yes to most of questions 1–5, then you are probably dangerously close to being a BD. If you answered yes to most of questions 6–10, then you are probably a DD.

Your goal should be becoming a Visionary Leader. This is crucial to transform yourself and your organization, and it requires strong self-esteem and the willingness to share and allow people to be part of a greater and better business or organization. Michael Gerber of eMyth fame calls this "working more *on* your business than *in* your business."

Becoming a Visionary Leader means developing the mission and vision of your business or organization. Ask yourself and your team what you stand for, what's your added value, who is your targeted audience, why should they do business with you, and so on. Including your people in these questions is important for them to feel like they are part of an idea or a vision, which will allow them to buy into the process. Without buy-in, you don't get their commitment, and with out commitment they won't take responsibility.

Here is the formula: Engage Your People = Get Buy-In = Commitment = Taking Responsibility.

Next, define the steps needed to implement the vision. If for example, you intend to go national with your product, or if you intend to sell on the Internet, define the steps and then decide who will be responsible and how will you evaluate the progress (e.g., weekly meetings, which we highly recommended, or weekly reports to keep everyone focused). Weekly meetings are very important for this process to work, as it allows all those that need to know, to know and it allows the boss to get full updates without having to nag or send emails every few minutes and it allows for group accountability to take form. More importantly, it allows for recognition to take place.

A great system that TAB (The Alternative Board) recommends and I have found that works is to, with your team, define your goals, strategies and action plans. This is called the Strategic Plan Process. It sounds simple, but it's not.

The goals are defined as the top five things the organization wants to accomplish within the next year, broken down by months. Usually I find that the two top goals are increasing the top line (sales or revenues) and the bottom line (net profit or Ebit -earnings before interest and taxes). That's a great start. Next, discuss the various strategies that can be employed to reach these goals. The strategies can be pages long, and they can be a combination of different lengths of time, from the short-term to the long-term.

The next step is the most crucial, and is the action plan. Identify every step that you must take to reach the goals. Identify who is responsible for the outcomes and by when does it need to be accomplished. This action plan should be updated by the most competent and organized person on staff and be the basis for the weekly meetings or reports. The action plan creates accountability and allows for continuous updates to the progress. The responsibility of the leader becomes keeping people accountable for achieving the goals, and more importantly giving the necessary recognition to those who are doing a great job. Recognition is the least expensive way to motivate and keep people achieving great results. Use those weekly meetings to praise your team, and always remember "praise in public, criticize in private."

I had read Roy's book many years ago and was impressed with his insights and systems for helping people. Over time, Roy has met with many entrepreneurs in our communities and has helped many turn their organizations and their lives around. (See the foreword of this book.)

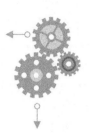

Chapter 14

ARE YOU A BAD BOSS?
"But I Never Yell!"

"Sometimes you're so good, you end up being good for nothing".
Barry Engel

	DIFFERENCES BETWEEN	
BOSS	**&**	**LEADER**
Drives employees		Coaches employees
Depends on authority		Depends on goodwill
Inspires fear		Generates enthusiasm
Says, "I"		Says, "We"
Places blame for the breakdown		Fixes the breakdown
Knows how it is done		Shows how it is done
Uses people		Develops people
Takes credit		Gives credit
Commands		Asks
Says, "Go"		Says, "Let's go"

W hen you think of the term "bad boss," what's the first thing that comes to mind? Annoying superiors who cut you down with remarks? Drill sergeants who yell at you in a fit of rage? Attention hogs that take credit for your work? Thoughtless task masters who hand out unexpected work to do over the weekend? You've been watching too many movies. Research suggests that most of the behaviors that we associate with bad bosses actually make up less than 20 percent of bad bosses.

The worst bosses, experts believe, are the ones who perform sins of *omission*, rather than sins of *commission*. In other words, being a bad boss is not about the horrible things that you do, but about the positive leadership activities that you *don't* do (however, it is worth noting that Jack Welch could not stand any manager who was a bully or a screamer. Remember, he looked for leaders with the 4E's of Leadership, which includes the ability "to articulate a vision and getting others to carry it out").

Let's take Nathan's experience as an example. Nathan was one of the nicest people I ever knew. So when he came to ask me, "Why is it that my people are not motivated and just do as they please?" I asked him if it would be OK for me to speak to some of his managers about it.

What I uncovered was that he wasn't setting significant goals with them; he was just accepting whatever they did as the maximum they could achieve. Instead of spending time and seriously thinking about how they could exercise their potential, he wanted to be Mr. Nice Guy. So he'd just let his managers and employees set their own performance level, and that is what he got.

I explained to Nathan that a boss really has to understand and involve himself in the strategic planning process, so that his employees understand that "reaching for the stars and landing on the moon" should be the norm, not the exception, as we covered in chapter 10.

But Mr. Nice Guy isn't the only bad boss out there. Experts have compiled a list of ten of the worst things a boss can do if he wants to be successful. Note how many of them are sins of *omission*:

1. **Lack of energy and enthusiasm.** This was the most noticeable of all the failings. An inspirational leader inspires his team. Without infectious energy, everyone just coasts through the week until payday.

2. **Lack of a clear vision.** If the leader doesn't have a clear path, his subordinates are left wandering aimlessly. It's the boss's job to give everyone direction.

3. **Lack of expectations.** If a boss doesn't encourage excellence, he's going to get mediocrity.

4. **Lack of guidance.** A good leader helps guide his subordinates to become better at what they do. He should be seen as more than a boss—he should be seen as a mentor and teacher. If the boss doesn't want every member of the team to grow, then he's kind of selfish, seeking only his *own* success, rather than the team's success.

5. **Lack of skills necessary to be a team player.** Poor leaders see the company as a competition in which only one person can eventually rise to the top seat. And he's sure not going to help anyone get a foothold over *him*. So he keeps things in his head, avoids his subordinates whenever possible, and doesn't communicate as much as he should.

6. **Lack of interpersonal skills.** Worse than not being a team player, these bosses are rude. They yell and demean others, and it's hard to imagine that they're good people even *outside* the office. Yes, this sounds like a sin of *commission*, but it can also manifest itself as *omission*. They don't reach out, they don't listen when others speak, and they don't praise or reinforce good performance.

7. **Lack of follow-through.** Some bosses don't practice what they preach. They say one thing and do another, losing the respect and trust of everyone around them. At best, their subordinates will try to behave as they do to get ahead, and eventually that laziness will be the entire face of the company.

8. **Lack of acceptance of new ideas.** If the suggestion isn't theirs, it's no good, even if the old ways are failing.

9. **Lack of good judgment.** These bosses make bad decisions and lead everyone into the river with them.

10. **Lack of learning from mistakes.** These bosses are so arrogant they fail to recognize past problems and admit a mistake, so the problems continue again and again.

Most of these flaws are difficult to see, as they all describe things that were *not* done, rather than things that *were* done. There's nothing explicit about these managers' behavior that draws attention to them. (In other words, it's far easier to come to the conclusion that there's oatmeal in the cabinets than to come to the conclusion that there isn't.) This means that, as a boss, you can be travelling down a road right now with no hint that anything is wrong, unless you take the time to think about your actions (or lack thereof) and look through your cabinets.

So what *should* you be doing? Ask yourself is if you possess the following three important skills:

1. **Trust.** Do your team members trust you? Do they know that you will stand up for them no matter what? Do you trust them? Do you tell them that you trust them? Trust empowers people; it gives them the courage to innovate, take risks, and to push themselves beyond their comfort zones to find success.

2. **Empathy.** Do you notice if your employee is having a bad day or going through a hard time? When was the last time you asked a co-worker that you thought something might be troubling them? Or are you too busy with your own agenda to notice? Do you treat your team members as human beings, rather than worker bees? Emotional intelligence is widely recognized as a leadership quality. Knowing that a boss cares is a fundamental human need.

3. **Mentorship.** No matter how talented and trustworthy a worker may be, she still needs guidance. She needs a mentor who will teach her the rules of the game and how to get better at it. There's no great worker who shouldn't be coached. Would you be where you are today

if your first manager hadn't shown you the ropes? Did you ever ask a worker if they would like a mentor? Mentorship is crucial when workers are unsure what the future holds. But you know what the future holds. You've been there.

So how do you go about building Trust, Empathy and Mentoring? Trust is built by being trustworthy and trustworthiness is built by being efficient and effective or by doing things right and doing the right thing. The reason why I highly recommend the 7 Habits to all my clients is because it's so foundational for creating trust and trustworthiness with your team and within your team. You need a foundation in order to build your business or organization, no different than needing a foundation to building a house. Imagine building a house without a foundation? How long will it last? How high can you build? Not too long and not too high. So if you're finding yourself in the same place over and over again, many times it's because there is no foundation.

Empathy or Emotional Intelligence is a huge and important skill, and to understand your and other's emotions, are essential for developing empathy. There are many tests that you can take to determine your level of empathy. It's especially important for those managers or leaders that are Guardians or STJ/P's (see chapter 1), as by nature they use their logical thinking brain and can forget to tap into their empathy in order to be a more effective leader.

In some of the leadership courses, I have been involved with, everyone gets a mentor. It's usually someone who has done the training before and has experience in their particular field and is willing to commit to a certain time per week/month in mentoring others. It's very effective and non-threatening to the mentee. In other trainings, we paired up with training partners and reviewed the weekly or monthly training and we'd practice with and on each other.

Chapter 15

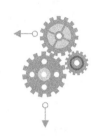

THE BUSINESS COACH:
Why Managers Need One

T he world of business is getting more competitive with each passing day, and it's difficult to keep up. Constant changes and innovations in sales, marketing, and management strategies make it important to have a business coach. It's not just a luxury anymore. You may be able to *survive* in business these days without the help of a coach, but it's almost impossible to *thrive*.

Business coaches are professionally trained advisers who guide others in developing and growing a business. They will help you clarify your goals and objectives and will direct you in developing skills and acquiring the resources you need to operate a successful enterprise. They will meet with you on a regular basis to discuss any and all business issues you are facing and will help give you clarity on how to create success.

It's very tricky to get a truly objective answer from yourself about your business, but your business coach will always tell you the truth, even if you don't want to hear it—especially when you don't want to hear it. He or she will provide you with valuable insight and can help you improve your business in areas that you might have overlooked.

Employees and managers will appreciate if you have a coach and feel more secure about the future of the business. They will feel that your decisions will be objective and well thought out.

Business owners will also benefit greatly when they are just starting up a business, as the day-to-day questions and decisions can be overwhelming.

For example, Jay was the shipping manager of a school-supply company. He requested that I coach him on starting his own business. He'd had quite a few years of experience and was anxious to open his own store. When he came to see me he confided that he was debating if he should become his own boss or work for someone else, because he was overwhelmed by the multiple responsibilities needed to start a business from scratch. How was he going to get financing, build a website, create a marketing campaign, sign up clients, keep control of his books and records, and so on? While in his current job he was successful in some of the functions like website design and his marketing plan, in other functions he needed help.

The first thing I had him do was take a Myers-Briggs Personality Test, and his results showed that he had good tolerance for risk and was very entrepreneurial, but he was easily distracted. When we put together a detailed business plan, I explained to him that his biggest challenge was not the financing, not the sales, but that he was too easily distracted.

As of writing this chapter, his plan is still not fulfilled, because—you guessed it! —He got distracted and jumped into something else. (Do you remember the lessons in chapter 8?) He now realizes that he made a mistake, and he is trying very hard to get back on track with the original plan. Without the guidance of a business coach, Jay might have never understood why he couldn't stick with his plan.

Coaching has become very popular these days, but many people are confused about the different types available. Personal or life coaching is very different from business and executive coaching. A personal coach or life coach focuses on the client's personal life, personal issues, and personal goals. You can work with him or her on weight loss, personal time management, and relationship issues. A business coach might focus on *some* personal issues, but mostly in the context of how they relate to the business. While most of his concerns will be business related, he can also assist you in balancing your business life with your personal life. He will also listen to your problems and help you set goals and build your sense of self-worth and confidence by encouraging and motivating you. And he'll keep tabs on your progress, requiring you to carry out and implement your plans. This accountability is one of the greatest strengths of working with a coach.

Executive coaches, on the other hand, are usually provided to senior managers, CEOs, directors, and business owners who want to take their awareness, learning, and development to the next level. Unlike business coaching, which is solution-focused, an executive coach will encourage you to find the solutions on your own. She will work to deepen your awareness of your specific challenges and help you analyze the various components of the issues at hand. This will help you gain fresh perspectives and enhance your thinking and decision making to solve the problem yourself. And unlike a business coach, she is unlikely to require the same level of exposure to as many areas of the business.

Here is an example of how working with an executive coach can help organize and streamline your workflow to make you more productive and successful. Ed was asked to take over as director of a very large health-care organization. While his expertise was not in health care, the board felt he could handle it. He asked me to be his executive coach so he could quickly learn the ins and outs of the organization and understand the challenges and how to respond effectively.

I helped him analyze the people and the structure of the organization—who reports to whom and what changes would be necessary. We came to the conclusion that the problem was that there were way too many people reporting to him, and that was bogging down his work.

We decided to implement a "Jethro type of management change," a restructuring of the organization into divisions with division heads who could be responsible for most decisions. We also established a very clear accountability program with the department heads by requiring clear progress reports and weekly management meetings. (The name of this action is based on a biblical story found in Exodus 18:13–23. After Moses had begun to lead the Israelites on their exodus, Jethro encouraged him to appoint others to share in the burden of ministry to the nation Israel by allowing others to help in the judgment of smaller matters coming before him.) Without an executive coach, Ed might have been successful, but he certainly would not have been as productive. Furthermore, the reorganization of the company helped to give structure and direction to the employees, and it also offered them more opportunities.

Business coaches may have different areas of expertise:

- **General-planning coaches** work with you on developing your strategic planning, your general administration and personnel issues, your marketing and promotional planning, and your financial management.
- **Marketing– and promotional-planning coaches** specialize in helping you develop and implement your promotional plan, advertising plan, and public-relations plan.
- **Financial-planning coaches** specialize in helping you understand financial statements, cash-flow management, pricing strategies, and employee compensation plans. (However, this type of business coach is not a tax adviser.)

Before meeting with a coach, check out his or her credentials:

- He should have extensive experience at the senior level of an organization.
- A good business coach should be professionally trained by a recognized coaching school.
- He should be able to identify and solve issues.
- He has to be a good motivator who can encourage you to accept challenges and overcome difficulties.
- He should be genuinely interested in people and have a desire to help others.
- He should be able to effectively communicate and listen.

- He will make you feel comfortable that he will inspire you to reach your fullest potential.

Most coaching partnerships begin with a lengthy start-up session of at least two hours, during which the coach will ask all about your history, your business, and your home life. The coaches also provide a contract, of course, and some other tools to get you started.

They key to an effective partnership between you and your coach is respect and trust. There must be a commitment by both parties to communicate and be loyal to each other, to spend the time working on your relationship and to establish a good rapport.

The best athletes have coaches because they are constantly improving, learning, and refining their skills. Every manager and leader needs to have a coach that they can bounce ideas off and help them keep to their goals. A great CEO will hold their people accountable, but who will hold the CEO accountable? It's the coach!

PART 5

MAXIMIZING OUR RELATIONSHIPS WITH OTHERS

Chapter 16

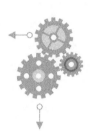

THE EMOTIONAL BANK ACCOUNT:
Balance Your Transactions

Emotional Bank Account

*And if you build a high reserve,
you can take more withdrawals.*

W e all know what a financial bank account is; it's where you keep your finances. If you make deposits, you can make withdrawals. If you take out more than you deposited, you have overdrawn your account.

This is also true in your relationships with your family, friends, colleagues, workers, boss, and others. You have an emotional bank account. A deposit in the account is anything that brings you closer together, and a withdrawal is anything that pushes you apart. For example, if you are criticizing your spouse and putting them on the defensive, even when you're right, you are withdrawing from the account. However, if you make a contribution to their account either by continuously complimenting your spouse or by not being critical, then you have made enough deposits to balance your account.

You don't want to make withdrawals at all, ideally, but life happens, and sometimes you have other priorities, and you have to disappoint. The goal, though, is to make as many deposits as you can to allow for the inevitable withdrawals. If you have very small deposits and huge withdrawals, the account will be wiped out. An argument with serious withdrawals might be where one person uses phrases like, "you always" or "you never." These accusations create defensiveness. However, if the person prefaces their criticism with phrases like, "most of the time your work is excellent, however it seems that this time something happened, can you explain," or "it seems you might not have been aware of these requirements." These types of phrases aren't necessary a withdrawal. Making deposits also requires first understanding what that person deems a deposit. For a spouse it might be compliments or quality time together; for an employee it might mean recognition of jobs well done. You can ask them!

Coach Bob Starkey, in talking about the emotional bank account, posted this story that illustrates what it means when we talk about making emotional deposits. He had a friend whose son developed an avid interest in sports. One summer, he took his son to see every major-league team play one game each. The trip took over six weeks and cost a great deal of money. But money wasn't the point. It was the shared experience that counted, and it became a powerful bonding experience in their relationship.

Upon return from his long trip, Starkey said to his friend, "I had no idea you liked sports that much." "I don't," he replied, "but I like my son that much." The time that this man and his son spent together was an investment in their relationship. That summer is something his son will never forget, so as a deposit in the emotional bank account, it is something that his son will be able to draw on for years to come.

Six Major Deposits

According to Stephen Covey, there are six ways you can make deposits in an emotional bank account.

1. **Understand the individual**. Each person has his or her own preferences about what kinds of activities and actions on your part would make emotional bank account deposits. While there are some general approaches that work for most people, it's important to know what makes a difference to each recipient. In fact, the very act of taking time to listen and learn what is important to each person is itself a big deposit in his or her emotional bank account—listen before we respond; diagnose before we prescribe. So if you have a direct report and you are looking to build trust, then asking them questions like, "How do you want to be managed (daily or weekly meetings)?" or "What communication style do you prefer (Continuous or end of day wrap up)?" or even ask, "What makes you feel valuable to our organization?" People will be honest with their needs if asked in a respectful way.

2. **Making and keeping commitments.** Once we know what kinds of deposits will resonate with the other person, the next step is to make commitments—and to keep those commitments. Every relationship has obligations to the other person, such as the obligation of a husband to let his wife know when he's going to be late. Or let's say you tell a major client that you will have something ready at a specific time. If you do not apprise him of a schedule change and don't deliver on time, you're making a huge withdrawal. Giving your word is a big deal, but only if you keep it.

3. **Clarifying expectations.** One of the biggest challenges we face as managers is making sure our expectations are clear. For example, if someone comes in for an interview, and we describe the job as "doing

everything that's needed in the office," we have not been very clear. But if we give them a clear job description—for example, "making phone sales, handling customer requests, mailing samples, and following up with quotes"—our expectations are clear, and we can later give specific feedback and praise success where appropriate.

4. **Remember that little things are big things.** A smile, a warm greeting on a cold morning, going the extra mile—these are all little positive things, but they add up to big deposits in people's emotional bank account. Take time for the small stuff. Employees remember when their employers have gone out of their way to show kindness and appreciation.

5. **Showing personal integrity.** An emotional bank account is all about trust. So just like making and keeping commitments, it's important to show personal integrity in every relationship. For example, don't talk about employees behind their backs, especially with other employees. The message it sends to the people you're talking to is that when they are not there, you will likely talk about them in the same way. Integrity is the foundation for any good relationship, and you will make big emotional bank account deposits when people see your personal integrity at work. Too many times we set the bad example of "do as I say and not as I do." Instead, you have to be able to "walk the talk."

6. **"You" and "I."** Another huge way of making deposits, or at least avoiding withdrawals, is to use *I*, rather than *you*. In other words, instead of saying, "You did something wrong," you can say, "I feel that this is wrong." When we use *you*, it often comes off as an evaluation and criticism of the person's character, and it makes the other person feel defensive. Giving feedback in the right way is a great way to build relationships. Talking about your needs or feelings shows vulnerability, which makes you more open and accessible to the other person. So even if a boss says something embarrassing to you in a meeting, telling them (in private) that it embarrassed you and that *you* would prefer that such things not be

said in public is more powerful and positive than accusing *them* of humiliating you.

A great way to accomplish all six points is to follow these three steps, whether you're dealing with a company, an organization, or even your own family:

1. **Refer to your mission statement.** Reflect back to chapter 9, where I elaborated on ways to craft your personal or professional mission statement. By now, you should have identified what kind of business or organization you want to be. For example, what qualities define your company? What kinds of feeling do you want in your organization? How do you want to build relationships? Use your mission statement as a guideline for what constitutes deposits. If your organization values maintaining their commitments, then know that each time you follow through, you are making a deposit in your customer's emotional account. Make sure that people understand the type of organization or family you want to create.

2. **Hold weekly meetings.** Gather your team once a week to talk about issues or problems, as well as to recognize what everyone is doing right. Refer to your mission statement to see how you are doing. Weekly meetings are the most powerful way to show recognition, inclusivity, transparency and accountability. Use these meeting effectively. Enjoy time together; do something fun.

3. **Remember the emotional bank account.** Again, this is similar to a financial bank account; you can make deposits to or withdrawals from each of your relationships. Make a conscious effort to make meaningful deposits in each one. When you make a withdrawal, apologize, and correct the mistake. Perhaps you can turn even the withdrawal into a deposit. Creating a balance scorecard for the organization might be a great way to keep track of how well people are interacting with each other. It's very beneficial to explain to each person on your team how you will create the feedback process. So,

for example, if there is one employee who dominates meetings and does not allow others to speak, a great way to give them feedback would be to tell them in private, "You might not be aware, but other members of the team feel overpowered, or spoken over, etc." Then in your meetings you might establish a two-minute rule, where people can only speak for two minutes, and then the next person speaks. Remember, praise in public (this will make deposits), and criticize in private (this will minimize the withdrawal).

Chapter 17

DIAGNOSE BEFORE YOU PRESCRIBE:
Empathetic Listening

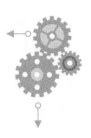

"Have an open mind to learn new things. If you only talk, then you are just repeating what you know, if you listen you will learn new things"
—Barry Engel

According to most communication experts, listening is a skill that needs to be learned and practiced to get it right. So what's so hard about listening? We need to learn to listen better, because we mostly listen with the intent to reply. We are so busy formulating the answers in our mind that we don't listen with the intent to understand first. Listening with the intent to understand is the greatest communication skill we can acquire.

Dale Carnegie said in *How to Win Friends and Influence People*:

> ...[I]f you aspire to be a good conversationalist, be an attentive listener. To be interesting, be interested. Ask questions that other persons will enjoy answering. Encourage them to talk about themselves and their accomplishments. Remember that the people you are talking to are

a hundred times more interested in themselves and their wants and problems than they are in you and your problems.

Being a good, *effective* listener far outweighs being the opposite. Talking too much without listening can have unintended and negative consequences. In the words of Calvin "Silent Cal" Coolidge, "No man ever listened himself out of a job."

According to Stephen Covey, there are five levels of listening:

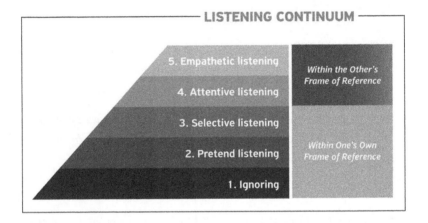

- Ignoring (I am making no effort to hear what you are saying.)
- Pretending (You think I'm listening, but I'm thinking about something else.)
- Selective listening (I hear part of what you're saying.)
- Attentive listening (I'm paying full attention.)
- Empathic listening (I fully *understand and feel* what you're saying.)

Recently, a company brought together its salespeople and the owners to learn about of empathetic listening—listening with the intent to understand. They agreed that this was their challenge. In the Sandler sales training we spoke about the need to ask good questions for the purpose of really understanding the needs of the customers. Listening is difficult because in part we tend to believe that if we listen, it means we agree. But we can say, "I hear you" or "I understand you," and that doesn't mean you have agreed. Once the person feels understood, then you can get them to understand you.

A manager and, more importantly, a leader should evaluate their listening skills. Understanding and listening to your employees is the most effective way will build trust and make deposits in their emotional bank account. It will also allow you to really know what's going on. Too many leaders isolate themselves in their ivory towers and don't spend enough time walking around talking and listening to their employees, managers, and customers. Steve Jobs was excellent at what is called MBWA (Manage by Walking Around). It allowed him to be in touch and know what was going on.

An effective salesperson seeks to understand the needs, concerns, and situation of the customer. An amateur sells products; a professional sells solutions. When Anne Mulcahy took the reins of Xerox, on the advice of Warren Buffett she spent a lot of time meeting with both customers and front-line employees to understand their wants and needs, which allowed her to turn the company around. So the next time you have an irate customer or employee, try using the following steps to get to empathetic listening.

Diagnose before You Prescribe

It can be dangerous to prescribe without an accurate diagnosis. As Roy Cammarano said, "Prescription without diagnosis is considered malpractice." In conversation, diagnosis is understanding, and prescription is response. To get a diagnosis, practice empathic listening by doing the following three steps.

1. *Give the person you are connecting with your full attention.* Remember that the person in front of you is your sole focus at this moment in time. Multitasking can be a great thing, but it's not appropriate when working empathically with another person, particularly when practicing empathic listening. I knew of a school principal that would unplug his phone when speaking to students, which demonstrated that they were getting his full attention.

2. *Do not speak when the other person is in the middle of communicating her issue.* Empathic listening means that it is your job to actually hear

what is being said and to reach the heart of the topic to achieve full understanding of the situation. In doing this you need to find out specifics, such as who is involved, what the actual problem is, and what the extenuating circumstances that encircle the problem are. All of this information can help you come up with the best-informed resolution you can offer. Without empathetic listening you might miss an intrinsic part of the problem. Peter Drucker said "The most important part of communication is hearing what isn't said."

3. *When the speaker is done talking, offer a summary of what you have heard.* This means you take what you have heard and reword it, replying with a summarized version of what he has said. It doesn't need to be more than an outline that goes over the most key points. This affirms to him that you were listening and reaffirms to yourself what you heard. Always ask, "Is there anything more that you would like to say?"

Empathetic listening and asking good questions creates the trust and goodwill of your colleagues and anyone you are communicating with. It will help you understand your customers better and understand what you need to do in order to improve your business. You might also want to try this with a good client, one with whom you have a trusting relationship. Ask them what you can do to grow your business, what services or products they would be interested in, and how you can improve whatever you are doing.

As a leader or manager, encourage your team to be more empathetic with each other. Try to really understand what the person is saying; ask clarifying questions, instead of assuming that you understand what's going on. If you feel that a person is not listening to you, a good way to help them listen is to say something to the effect of, I really want to listen and understand what you have to say, and I'm sure you're interested in hearing what I have to say.

I was the Chair of a community-based project and was challenged with members that were constantly arguing and confronting each other. So we created a policy that before anyone could reply, they needed to repeat what they had heard, and the other party had to agree that those were the points.

It made a huge difference in the how members communicated, and people actually started understanding each other without jumping to conclusions.

As I quote my father that said "*have an open mind to <u>learn</u> new things. If you only talk, then you are just repeating what you know, if you listen you will learn new things*".

Chapter 18

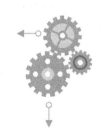

THE SECRET TO
SELLING SUCCESS:
Ask, and Listen

"Everyone can sell a dollar for 99 cents"
—Barry Engel

Whenasked what are the attributes of a great salesperson, most people will answer with one or more of the following:

- Product or service knowledge
- Good people skills
- Persistence
- Willingness to take a lot of rejection
- Knowledge that it's a numbers game (the more people you call on, the more you sell)
- Ability to get one's foot in the door
- Ability to get past the gatekeepers

While these are all true and are important skills, the most important and the most overlooked is the ability to ask good questions and listen. As a business owner or a manager, you might be need to talk to customers or train your people in sales, so understanding this principle and some of the others listed below will greatly enhance your and your team's success.

My partner Mervyn has a financial sales company, and he struggled to find good, qualified sales people. He asked me to look into different training programs and I found that Bob Heiss Sales methods from Sandler Training was very much based on the listening principles we mention above.

David Sandler, from Sandler Sales Systems, created an eight-step process for all types of sales. He claims that many people say they are willing to do "whatever it takes" to achieve a desired goal—until it's actually time to produce. To change and grow, you have to modify your behavior and do things differently than you've been doing them up until that point. If you've been functioning in your comfort zone, it is not easy to venture out, and it takes commitment to do what needs to be done *when* it needs to be done.

On the surface, selling appears to be an intellectual process: matching products and services with people who have a need for them. However, it's not that clear-cut and easy, and there are lots of emotions involved. You start by searching for the people who are in need of the products and services you're selling. These are people who are usually not interested in being interrupted from the task at hand and don't have the desire or time to engage in a conversation with you. The selling process, by its very nature, is filled with opportunity for rejection.

If you were a sales robot, you would be able to go from prospect to prospect without taking the rejection personally. But salespeople are human and, thus, wired with emotions. At some point, after experiencing one rejection after another, you will likely begin to interpret it as personal failure. "Why me?" "What am I doing wrong?"

For example, Michael, a salesman at a software development firm, walked into the office of a prospect and asked to see Ben Darby, the CEO. He launched into his sales pitch, but Mr. Darby interrupted him, saying, "I don't have time for this nonsense." He turned his back to Michael and began sorting through a pile of mail.

Michael tried catching Mr. Darby's attention to no avail and finally turned and walked out, deflated. He had started out the day feeling bright and optimistic, but after a sixty-second encounter with a stranger who didn't have the decency to be courteous, he was now feeling like a peddler—dejected and ready to abandon the prospecting.

Michael's reaction was emotional and is typical of many salespeople. Mr. Darby was likely having a bad day and was venting his frustration on Michael. But instead of ignoring Mr. Darby's reaction and moving on, Michael allowed himself to be drained of his confidence, courage, drive, persistence, and self-esteem.

Bear in mind that nobody can make you feel one way or another; your feelings are purely the result of your own thinking. Therefore, learning to look at the events differently is very important. (See chapter 4 about emotional intelligence) You are free to interpret events any way you want. You can give them a positive spin to create positive feelings or a negative spin to create negative feelings. You can look at the temporary setback as a learning experience and a challenge—an opportunity to develop a more innovative way. The choice is yours. You don't have to allow anyone to drain you.

David Sandler discovered that many people relate their self-worth to their job performance. If they perform well, they feel good about themselves, and if they don't, they feel they are worth less as a human being. The salespeople who achieve consistently high levels of success have high levels of self-esteem, regardless of the outcome of any particular sales challenge. They don't let occasional negative events tarnish their identity.

Imagine that your inner world and your emotions, especially when you're out selling exist in an elaborate castle. The doors are securely locked, and only you have the keys. In your castle you are safe. Your self-worth and value as a human being are protected from outside influences. Nothing from the outside can affect you.

Each day you don your armor—your confidence, courage, and self-esteem—and venture out. Frustrating and disappointing experiences may temporarily dent your armor, but at any time you can retreat into your castle, bolt the doors, and once again be safe and secure, with your self-worth intact. No one can harm you. The events of the outer world remain in the outer world. Your sales performance may have been lacking, but your value, as an individual has not been diminished one bit. With your self-worth intact, you can brush up on your sales techniques and learn how to present your sales pitch smoothly.

Understanding your own needs and emotions allows you to step back from the emotional side of the sales process and create a thought-out sales call that has all the elements well versed before going in. Otherwise, you can either be too unprepared and therefore vulnerable to a tough client, or you can become defensive, conniving, or only say what the client wants to hear in order to get the sale. These situations will create erratic and unpredictable results.

Sandler says that a major weakness in the sales paradigm is that when a company gets an inquiry or a salesperson goes out on a call, they focus on explaining the "features and benefits"—how their products have certain very important features and how those features have very important benefits. This might seem like a great idea, but it has its issues.

For example, Sol and Daniel were introducing a new computer-based educational tool for children with learning difficulties. The tool had had great success in other communities, and they believed it should be successful in more as well. These, however, were their challenges:

1. It was expensive, and people were reluctant to pay.
2. Whenever they ran an ad, it generated a huge amount of calls and inquiries from parents and educators, but not enough sales.

When they did the Sandler training, they realized they were focused on explaining to all their callers that their learning system had great features and benefits—better than all the systems out there. The problem was that those callers heard the same basic spiel from all the other companies selling similar systems. So they needed a way to differentiate themselves. In addition, they didn't have good ways for dealing with the price concerns and other common objections that people usually have, such as "I need to think it over," or "I have to ask my spouse."

The big challenge of explaining features and benefits is the problem of supplier shopping. Once the customer knows everything about the product, he now knows what to ask when he goes to the second supplier. All you are is a source of research he will use to get the best deal from your competitor. And if you're offering services, people want you to tell them what you do, how you do it, and what common issues you try to avoid. This gives them a lot of good ideas, and you end up doing a lot of unpaid consulting.

To overcome these problems, what you really need to do is 1) listen, 2) ask the right questions, and 3) listen again. Listening is an acquired skill, as we have already discussed. But to find something worth listening to, you have to ask the right questions.

What are the right questions?

The first thing you have to remember upon making a sale is that people are reluctant to change or make any step toward moving out of their comfort zone unless there is a compelling reason to do so. Many people create and live in a comfort zone. We know we should be doing certain things differently but there are reasons that we don't make the change. For example, I know I have to exercise and lose weight, but it requires commitment, time, discipline, and energy. Not spending any of these things allows me to stay in my comfort zone, but to get the results I want—a healthier lifestyle—I need to venture out of it. The same goes for the sales process. Sometimes even if your product is better and cheaper, the client is still reluctant to change. Why? Because it requires an effort; it requires things like money or time, or it invokes an emotion like fear (e.g., "Maybe my boss won't like it" or "Maybe it won't work as well"). So we do nothing. The diagram below shows more reasons why people are reluctant to move out of their comfort zones. The biggest one is Fear. It can be fair of failure, like someone said "if it ain't broke don't fix it". Another fear is what other people might say or think about you or your decision. See below for many other reasons people stay in their comfort zone.

Main Reasons People Say
It's Hard to Move out of
Their Comfort Zone

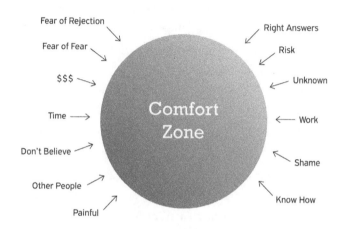

Recently, we trained a company that helped children with ADD/ADHD. They had a great computer-based product but no sales. When they switched from a benefits focus to really first understand the concerns and "pain" of the parent, they started to see sales increase. The more they understood their customers' problems, the more they sold. So when they asked a parent what their concerns with their child were, if the parent answered, for example, getting thrown out of school, they knew the pain was serious. They could then move on to other questions, like when they would like to start, if they had a budget, and who needed to approve it (e.g., their spouse or school). Sandler suggests that to be a great salesperson, you need to understand both the pain and gain points your client is having that got them to call you and the comfort zones they are hoping to get back to.

Here are some of the questions you might want to ask potential customers:

1. How long has this been a problem?
2. What are some of the things that have been tried?
3. Why didn't they produce results?

4. Is the problem big enough that you want to do something about it?

5. If yes, what is it you would like to do?

That last question is what we call the closing question, and it helps close the deal. In other words, understanding the problem and then explaining how you can help solves their problem gets them back to their comfort zone and allows you to sell them your solution.

Another important part of the listening sales process is understanding objections. Salespeople know they will get the typical brush-offs, for example, "I have to think it over," or I need to ask my boss/partner/spouse," or "Call me after the holidays." When you start to chase them, they hide. They don't return your calls or emails and you wonder what happened.

While the above statements are all valid and understandable, you need to ask your potential customers pointed questions. For example, "So what are you going to tell your partner/boss/spouse, and what do you think they will reply?" The one I like is when a prospect answers they need to think it over, you ask them the following question: "Most people, when they say they need to think it over, say it for one of two reasons. Either they have more questions, or they really want to say no but are not comfortable. Which one is it for you?"

Having a well-prepared script is a huge benefit in asking the right questions at the right time.

Aside from understanding your client's pain points, making others feel OK, versus not OK, is another major determinant of a successful outcome. As kids, we were soothed by our parents: "I know how you feel," "You'll be OK," "Don't worry; it's going to be all right." When we received these messages, we felt powerful, positive responses, including feelings of comfort, validation, acceptance, and safety. We felt OK.

The ability to evoke OK emotions is a major bonding tool. People are more likely to interact effectively and communicate better when they feel OK. Emotionally supportive messages arise from our nurturing parent and can take many forms, including supportive body language and facial expressions that encourage the other person to speak. Statements such as, "We've seen this kind of issue before," "I understand your frustration," and "That must have been a very difficult period for your company. Let's see what we can do to make sure it doesn't happen again," can open doors and make productive transactions possible. You have to be certain, though, that these messages are authentic and respectful. On the flip side, making the prospect or customer feel not OK is guaranteed to earn you zero sales. Lecturing or telling them what to do will lead them to dismiss you figuratively or literally.

Most people think of success in terms of accomplishments, such as winning a major account, reaching sales goals, winning sales awards, or getting promoted. These achievements are in actuality, however, *signs* of success and are the result of three core elements: attitude, behavior, and technique. The sales method teaches that we need all three elements to work together in order for success to become reality.

> **Attitude:** Your state of mind or feeling about yourself, your company, or your product is your attitude. It can be positive, leading to an outlook of possibility, or it can be negative, leading to an outlook of limitation. Most of our outlooks are self-imposed, and we can choose which one to have. We usually develop our attitudes based on previous experiences.

> The outlook you choose is the first step to create a self-fulfilling prophecy and will have a greater impact on your success than almost any other choice. Changing your outlook will start a chain reaction that will change your outcome.

> **Behavior:** Behaviors are driven by goals. Goals get you out of bed in the morning and motivate you to tackle the day's activities. Without them, you just go through the motions. You need clearly defined goals to determine what you want to do, and then you can develop an action plan for accomplishment.

> Focus on SMARTER goals: specific, measurable, attainable, relevant, time-bound, enjoyable, and rewarding. Be exact, and don't set up impossible goals. Make sure your goals are enjoyable and rewarding—something you'll look forward to achieving.

Once you have your goals in place, you can develop a plan for achieving them. Keeping a journal to track your daily goals and check up on yourself periodically is very helpful.

Technique: Your technique comprises your strategies, your plans, your tactics, and the actual moves you make to carry out your strategy. Mastering a technique involves being able to apply the right skills in the right situation.

Getting all three elements of the success triangle may take just a few minutes to understand but take a lifetime to master. Ask yourself and your team how your attitude, behaviors, and techniques are. Do you all sell from the same sell page? Have your salespeople been trained? Did you give them the necessary tools to succeed? If the answer is no, then you need to get out of your comfort zone.

Chapter 19

NEGOTIATION SKILLS:
Know What You Want, and Get It

"Know what you stand for and what you won't stand for"
—Jacob Engel

Another part of sales is negotiations, especially if your sales involve large or long-term contracts. Companies love to negotiate. As well as practicing the techniques from the previous chapter, this win-win mindset will help you and your team really excel. It can be used in salary negotiations as well as any interpersonal negotiations. Covey even taught this method successfully to heads of state.

Harvey Young from Covey did this exercise with our team, which you can practice with your team:

Ask everyone to split into groups of two and play tic-tac-toe. Tell them that their objective is to maximize the wins. Each team gets three tries.

Most of the time, you will find that the games end in a tie, as each side tries to win and not let the other person win. Two thinking adults playing tic-tac-toe will almost always end in a stalemate. But that's not what you told them to do. You didn't tell them to *win*, but to *maximize* the wins, meaning to make sure that each game has a winner, if not more than one. There are a few ways to maximize wins, including having each person stay on one side of the board and not get in each other's way, or having both players write Xs and neither of them write Os.

We are conditioned to think that if we win, someone else has to lose, and if someone else wins, we have to lose. Again, this is called the scarcity mentality. But there's really enough room on the board for two or even three people to get three in a row (or even for nine people, if everyone's putting down Xs). This is called the abundance mentality. The game is no longer so competitive, but that's kind of the point.

When it comes to negotiating a deal, we know that there are generally four ways it can end:

1. Win-win
2. Win-lose
3. Lose-win
4. Lose-lose

In other words, if the result is good for both parties, it's called a win-win. When it's good for me, but you don't get everything you want out of it, it's called a win-lose. When you get everything you want, but I don't, it's a lose-win. If neither of us is happy, it's a lose-lose. (The classic example of a lose-lose is when a husband wants to live in New York and his wife wants to live in Israel, so they buy a houseboat and set up camp in middle of the Atlantic.)

But what if, instead of visualizing four ways it can possibly end, there were only two ways: win-in or no deal? In other words, if the negotiations don't end with both people coming out winning, everyone should just take their business elsewhere.

That isn't easy. For example, to achieve anything on the top of the above chart, we would have to have an enormous amount of consideration for everything the other person wants. To achieve anything on the right side of the chart, we would have to have the courage to express everything that *we* want, despite what we think the other party's reaction might be. To achieve the top right quadrant, we need to be mature enough to have both courage and consideration.

For example, let's say a business owner is looking to hire a manager. The owner has been looking to hire for a while, and the manager has been looking for a job for a while. Because both parties are interested in getting it done, there is very little discussion about the exact details of the job description. A week into the job, however, the owner isn't very happy, and the manager isn't sure why.

If the company just backs down because they don't have the courage to confront the manager, it will be lose-win. If the company insists that it's their way or the highway, then it's a win-lose. For a win-win, both parties need to have the courage to review the details beforehand and make sure that it's what they are each looking for. Both need to have the consideration for each other that if it's not right, they should say no to the whole deal. Hiring the wrong person is very costly for companies, and firing is very costly for the employee (both financially and emotionally).

You can use the win-win or no deal framework to prepare for negotiations as well. For example, Esther was in the process of analyzing her career as a social worker. She was burned out by the many tough cases she was getting, and it seemed like she needed a career change. In our discussions with her, she identified that couple's counseling was something she really enjoyed. After researching her options, she met with a great group that was willing to offer her training and a career change, but it didn't completely match her needs. I met with her and suggested that she make a list of what was important in the job offer and what wasn't that important to her, and then understand what was important for them that she could offer. When she met with the group, she was able to articulate what a win-win would mean for her. She courageously continued to ask for, and eventually got, the important things, because she was considerate of what the organization needed from her. It meant that she had to negotiate for a while, but it worked out.

"Win-win or no deal" is a proactive approach that says we will do business together only if we can determine that it's a win for both of us. Otherwise, let's agree that we won't bother. This is a very powerful leadership tool that, when used sincerely and upfront, allows you to create and define the outline of the desired results.

Here is an example. I once negotiated with a bank a real estate refinancing deal, and the agreed upon guideline was that it should be a win-win for both of us. When we were ready to close the deal, the lawyer on the bank side surprised us with a huge pile of documents that needed to be signed in order for the bank to go ahead with the financing. We expected a refinance that mirrored the original deal, not a whole new financing negotiation. So I sat down with the bank executive and asked him if he believed that the bank's attorneys were thinking win-win or not. He agreed that they weren't, and we simplified the deal that was a win for both of us. It preserved our relationship and allowed us to have the courage to say no, and the bank was considerate enough to agree that it wasn't a win-win for both. The bank executive demonstrated the importance in a win-win mentality for a leader. He had the authority to override the attorneys' decision, and was thus able to close the deal as we both wanted.

Many people think in terms of either/or: you can be nice, or you can be tough. Win-win or no deal requires that you be both.

It's a balancing act between:

- Integrity and maturity,
- Courage and consideration, and
- Empathy and confidence.

I know that this is a hard balance to achieve, so I will offer you a win-win: if you are challenged in creating a win-win situation, feel free to contact me, and I'll help you achieve it at no charge.

Recently we helped an organization renew its contract with its employees using the win-win strategy. The partner in charge was determined to meet with each employee and work it out. The result was an empowered workforce with very clear responsibilities.

I recently received an email from her saying that "I just wanted to let you know what a difference it makes having open communication [and create a win-win agreement]. Sometimes it feels like I am not making any headway and then I get such a positive feedback and I think YES there is hope. I would also like to thank you for all your guidance in helping us make it happen".

Chapter 20

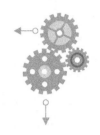

MAKING THE BEST DEAL:
Be a Savvy Leader

"The best deal with bad people will always be a bad deal"
—Paul Silberberg

M any people—sometimes even *smart* people—do very foolish things, especially with their money and investments. To paraphrase P. T. Barnum, "There's a fool born every minute."

Some people shrug off financial losses, say that it was not in their hands anyway, that maybe they were destined to lose money. Some people believe that even if they do foolish things, if they combine it with enough hope-for-the-best attitude, it will translate it into enormous profits anyway.

So what is it that compels people to get duped into lousy investments? Unfortunately, there are many scams and frauds. It's worthwhile to see through the too-good-to-be-true promises and understand how to invest wisely. If it's too good to be true, it's probably not true.

I know of many people that have invested millions of dollars in projects but have neglected to go see their investment, for example, or at least meet the people they're entrusting their money to. It's only after the deal goes sour that they say, "If only I would have known…."

Leaders need to be savvy in making sure they are dealing with honest and reputable people. Sometimes a leader needs to be able to say no to a shady deal or one that as someone called it the New York Times test. Meaning if it makes it to the front page of the NY Times, would you have done the deal?

There are a lot of schemes out there, and it's important to watch your step. Here are two to the famous ones:

1. **The "Nigerian prince" scheme:** You receive an offer from supposed Nigerian royalty promising big profits in exchange for help moving large sums of money out of his country. "If only you give us your bank account information and some initial money to help us get this moving…." No offense, but real Nigerian princes don't need you.
2. **The Ponzi scheme:** Ponzi scheme organizers solicit money by promising to invest in opportunities with high returns and no risk. Most of the time, there actually is *no* investment opportunity; they're just pocketing the money. But to show how much profit they're "making," the fraudsters give the investors some "returns," actually consisting of money from *other* people tricked into investing. Bernie Madoff is probably the most recently notorious Ponzi schemer, but the SEC investigates many such cases every year.

Yet interesting enough, each year people fall into these scams because they don't watch for the dangers signs.

However, the purpose of this chapter (and the message of this book) is to talk about extremely successful leaders who have demonstrated over and over that their honesty, integrity, and trustworthiness are not for sale at any price. These are real people that I have come across—yes, real *mentschen*—and their word is their word.

Paul is one of the most astute investors I have come across, yet his most important trait is his honesty and integrity. His motto is "The best deal with bad people will always be a bad deal." This is the axiom he lives by, which is featured on his website. He says, "We have found that our greatest asset is our credibility. Our business strategy is to under promise, over perform, and do whatever it takes for both our clients and our community."

Jordan is another extremely successful and savvy investor. His website says, "[Our] companies, [which are] of the highest integrity, foster an environment of mutual collaboration, inspiring loyalty among the companies, employees, customers, and investors. With an emphasis on fairness and the highest ethical standards, [we] create an environment promoting teamwork and innovation."

Now, I can tell you that both have made bad judgment calls at some point, and both have had their ups and downs. But the key to their ultimate success was in how they handled it.

Paul once sent a letter to his investors that read something like this: "We have recently put money in a project that then turned out to be a bad investment. We realize that our due diligence was not according to our regular standards. Therefore, we are returning all the investors' monies, plus all fees associated with this deal." He personally visited his investors in their offices to explain the current tough market conditions and what his company was doing about it. He also told me that when he had to lay off employees, he couldn't sleep at night, because these people had been so loyal to him, and he felt terrible doing what needed to be done. It shows the incredible balance in being an astute investor and returning great results to your clients yet having a great sense of loyalty and responsibility when things aren't going so well.

Jordan has demonstrated his savvy in tough markets, and he has even grown his business in a period when others were failing. Recently he made a huge deal, which yielded unbelievable returns for his clients, but he was very careful to explain to everyone that it was an anomaly and should not be the basis of future investments. He says, "No one likes someone who under delivers by making promises that are overly optimistic." Too many leaders will believe in their own hubris and take their successes as something which they can repeat over and over. There is a well know saying that "pride cometh before the fall". Being humble is a great trait for the successful and prosperous leader.

A successful investment firm is not one that always picks winners. It's one that handles even the losing investments with integrity and feeling for everyone who has put their faith in the firm.

The most important traits that a savvy leader can learn and use are:

- Be humble.
- Take ownership of any problems (e.g., "the buck stops here").
- Have a deep understanding of your business.
- Hire the best people you can afford.
- Hope for the best, yet prepare for the worst.
- Know what you stand for and what you won't stand for.

The savvy leader is the one that combines all the best attributes of honesty, integrity, compassion with a clear purpose and mission, empowering their people yet remaining humble and appreciative of the many people that have helped them achieve great success.

I'm particularly fond of Covey's reflection in his book about attending a funeral "your own" funeral and asking, what is it you want people to say about you?

When my father passed away one of his accountants, Ernie Wilkens, attended and said something that was very telling of his charitable nature. He said that each year he would review the donations to charity and say, "Barry, again you gave away more money to charity that you should have". To which my father would reply "Ernie, G-D willing we will make more money next year and give away even more to charity".

I remember attending an Investor's seminar years ago, at which the founder of Home Depot spoke about charitable endeavors. He said, "you need to work as hard giving away your money as making your money".

PART 6

PREPARING FOR A BRIGHTER FUTURE

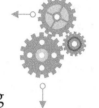

Chapter 21

A LIFE OF MEANING:
The Key to Happiness and Well-Being

*The happiest people
don't have the best of everything,
they just make the best
of everything.*

When we hear the word *happy*, we perk up and think of merriment, ebullience, good cheer, and smiles. However, happiness today is a fuzzy concept. Feeling cheerful or merry is a far cry from real, lasting inner happiness. Millions of dollars have gone to waste in the pursuit of happiness; they have failed to yield significant results.

Hollywood and Madison Ave are the epitome of making us spend a lot to "buy happiness." They tell us that if we buy W and drive X, or we vacation in Y and wear label A, then we will feel happy forever. We tend to choose what makes us feel good in the moment, but it's very important to realize that too often our choices are not made for the sake of how we will feel long term.

Modern conceptions of happiness are misleading because the focus is in the wrong place. Today happiness is viewed as a mood, a feeling that passes. This understanding isn't wrong as much as it is shortsighted. Moods shift and feelings change. While feeling happy may differ from day to day, if the overall direction of your life has provided you with feelings of contentment, peace, and real joy, you can be happy in the deeper and more permanent sense.

If you are in business, achieving a state of well-being may be particularly relevant to you. People who are happier are very often more successful at work as well. Research shows how satisfaction and happiness are connected to higher success rates and productivity, as well as better business outcomes. And many of the principles and habits that make for a happy and satisfying life are directly applicable to building a happier and more effective culture within your business.

Employees and managers are affected by how the leaders look and act, especially in crisis. One of the most important traits of leadership is being calm under stress. We quoted Warren Buffett, who said that mental stability is the most important attribute a leader needs. Happy managers make happy employees, who in turn make happy customers.

Everyone wants to be happy, yet we spend our days with our noses to the grindstone, trying to achieve happiness we'll never have time to enjoy. At no point will we ever step back and say, "That's enough working. I can enjoy the results now."

It's well worth investing the effort in attaining true happiness. When we are happy, we are less self-focused, we tend to like others more, and we are more open to share our good fortune with others. When we are down, on the other hand, we become distrustful, turn inward, and focus exclusively on our own needs. Consequently, withdrawing from others puts an even bigger distance between ourselves and the happiness we seek.

Studies have proven how being socially connected affects a person's well-being, while lacking social ties increases depression and negative affectivity. A happy person makes a delightful companion, friend, parent, and employee. People are attracted to someone who radiates positive energy and joy, and being constantly surrounded by friends and family makes a happy person even happier.

Martin Seligman, the father of positive psychology, conducted extensive research on how extremely happy people differ from the rest of us. The results were that they were extremely social. They each had a meaningful relationship, were involved in group activities, and often had a rich repertoire of friends. Seligman has written extensively on the topics of learned optimism, authentic happiness, and flourishing, in which he details his findings on how to achieve well-being and happiness. He disliked the disease model, where psychologists and psychiatrists have become "pathologizers" and "victimologists" and have forgotten that people have responsibility and can make choices. They haven't developed interventions to make people happy, and they have forgotten about improving normal lives and increasing talents and creativity.

Seligman strongly believes that we should be just as concerned with strengths as with weaknesses and just as interested in building the best things in life as repairing the worst. This can help make the lives of normal people more fulfilling and nurture talent and genius. His theory is that happiness can be broken down into three different elements: positive emotions, engagement, and meaning.

Positive emotions are what we feel, such as pleasure, ecstasy, warmth, and the like. They come from doing things that we enjoy and that make us feel good, like reading a good book or listening to great music. We learn to amplify positive feelings by savoring them as much as we can. An entire life led around these pleasurable sensations is called the pleasant life.

The second element, engagement, is what Mihály Csíkszentmihályi calls "flow." It is characterized by complete absorption in what one does and is the feeling of time stopping, a loss of self-consciousness when completely absorbed in something. In a sense, engagement is the opposite of positive emotions; when you ask people who are in flow what they are feeling, they say, "Nothing." In flow, we merge with the object of our attention, such as a project or a game; the concentrated attention that it requires uses up all the cognitive and emotional resources that make up thought and feeling. In order to go into flow it's important to identify your highest strengths and learn to use them more often. It requires re-crafting your life based on your strengths.

In the now popular field of positive psychology, the greatest importance is helping people understand their strengths and building their career around it. Managers and leaders alike should take the time to understand what motivates their people, and the greatest motivator is doing what you really feel energized by. I'm in the process of becoming a positive psychology coach. One of the main reasons is because it's extremely gratifying to help people understand themselves and follow their calling.

The third and most significant element of happiness is meaning. The pursuit of pleasure and engagement are often solitary endeavors. Human beings, ultimately, need meaning and purpose in life. Meaning can come from using your highest strengths in the service of something you perceive as bigger than yourself. Refer to my past quotations of Victor Frankl and others who have said that meaning and purpose is the most gratifying work that man can do.

> *"Choose a job you love, and you will never*
> *have to work a day in your life".*
> **—Confucius**

The drawbacks to the pleasant life are, first, that it's hard to change. Second, it habituates, meaning you adjust to it fast and the pleasure decreases. For example, when licking an ice-cream cone, in the first taste you get 100 percent pleasure, but by the sixth taste the pleasure is almost gone. So the pursuit of pleasure makes almost no contribution to happiness. Engagement and meaning are what contribute most to happiness, with meaning taking first place. When you have that, pleasure is like the cherry on top.

Seligman believes that each person possesses several signature strengths. Strengths are traits, not just one-time actions. They are virtues and are valued in their own right in almost all cultures. He compiled a list of strengths that can be measured. Among them are wisdom and knowledge, spirituality and transcendence, love and humanity, courage, justice, and temperance. These are strengths of character that a person self-consciously owns, celebrates, and can exercise every day in many areas of life. The idea is to use your signature strengths every day in the main realms of your life to bring authentic happiness.

When a leader uses their strengths and encourages others to do the same, it creates a lot of positive energy. People feel good about doing what they do well, and that creates a positive energy culture. Recently I worked with an organization that struggled with keeping their good employees motivated. It required many meetings based on a win-win outcome that allowed these employees to articulate their need to feel important and empowered, which resulted in them taking ownership of many executive functions, which in turn freed the executives to do greater things.

To have a meaningful life is to use your strengths and virtues in service of something bigger than yourself. The larger the system you attach yourself to, the more meaning you get out of life. There are lots of pre-packaged systems as well—systems such as family, religion, political parties, and the like—that can help you find meaning.

Then there are jobs, careers, tasks, and so forth that you are already engaged in but don't see much meaning in. Converting your ideas about them, however, can result in a more meaningful life. For example, being a lawyer can either be a business just in service of making half a million dollars a year, in which case it's not meaningful. Or it can be in service of good counsel, fairness, and justice; that's a meaningful life.

There are other ways to live a meaningful life. You need to examine your values, beliefs, strengths, and talents to determine in which direction to go. According to Seligman, gratitude and doing something altruistic are among the top on the list. Gratitude is the ability to be keenly aware of the good things that happen to you and never take them for granted. Grateful individuals express their thanks and appreciation to others in a heartfelt way, not just to be polite. If you possess a high level of gratitude, you often feel an emotional sense of wonder, thankfulness, and appreciation for life itself.

Researchers are finding that individuals who exhibit and express the most gratitude are happier, healthier, and more energetic. In various studies, grateful people reported fewer physical and emotional symptoms such as headaches, stomachaches, depression, anxiety, and stress. On the flip side, when an individual has an insufficient appreciation of good events and an overemphasis of bad or unfortunate experiences, contentment and satisfaction with life are greatly undermined.

A simple way to improve your gratitude is to write down five things for which you felt grateful for, once a week, for ten weeks in a row. Exciting results will emerge. Students that did the experiment reported feeling less stressed and more content, optimistic, and satisfied with their life. It's interesting to note that while counting your blessings on a regular basis can improve mood and overall level of happiness and health, expressing that appreciation to others will do so even more. Even noticing, appreciating, and expressing our feelings for life's *little* blessings can produce just as much benefit as noticing the monumental moments.

Although we may acknowledge gratitude's benefits, it can still be difficult to feel grateful when we are going through a difficult time. It may be human nature to notice all that is wrong or that we lack, but Dan Gilbert, a Harvard Psychology Professor and author of *Stumbling on Happiness*, challenges the idea that we'll be miserable if we don't get what we want. Our "psychological immune system" lets us feel truly happy, even when things don't go as planned.

He claims that our beliefs about what will make us happy are often wrong, and he says that natural happiness is what we feel when we get what we wanted, while synthetic happiness is what we make of when we don't get what we wanted. In our society, we have a strong belief that synthetic happiness is of an inferior kind, that putting a good spin on a bad situation or being a good loser is just a way to save face, but that is not the case at all. He supports this premise with intriguing research. (www.ted.com/talks/dan_gilbert_asks_why_are_we_happy.html)

Altruism is another thing that can greatly affect the level of meaning in your life. By doing things to benefit others, you will become a much happier person. For example, volunteering just one day a month can give your life a greater sense of purpose and can make you feel more connected to your community. There's a significant correlation between well-being and volunteer work. Think you're too busy? It's not about how much time you give, but about forming an identity as a volunteer. Many companies see the value of giving employees one-day paid leave for volunteer work, or they match donations, all for the purpose of creating altruistic and compassionate employees.

There are many different ways in which you can help others: being a listening ear to a friend; helping a friend or neighbor who is ill; doing something for someone else that requires time and effort on your part. One day each week, commit five random acts of kindness, and when possible, make them anonymous.

Following are more suggestions that can increase meaning in your life:

- **Creating:** Writing, drawing, painting, playing music, inventing something, building a business, coming up with a clever marketing campaign, and forming a nonprofit are all ways of contributing to the world in a positive way will give you a greater feeling of significance.
- **Relating:** It's not "family" that makes life worth living, but the relationships we create with members of our family and the way we maintain and build those relationships. The same goes for friends, business partners, students, and everyone else.
- **Playing:** Letting go of restraints, imagining new possibilities, testing yourself against others or against yourself, and finding humor and joy can all help you stay feeling positive about life, no matter what situation you're in.
- **Growing:** Learning new things or improving knowledge and ability in the things you've already learned help you to constantly feel renewed and are a way to continue to grow.

Finding meaning in your life isn't hard, but it's definitely harder than living a fast-paced, superficial life. Make the decision to start your search for meaning, and experience everything that life has to offer. You won't regret it.

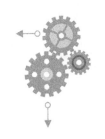

Chapter 22

REINVENTING YOURSELF:
"Make the Rest of Your Life
the Best of Your Life" —Brian Tracy

With hundreds of thousands of professionals across the United States taking early retirement or being laid off, people in all walks of life are struggling to figure out what to do next. How will they pay the mortgage and feed their family if their savings or pension is insufficient? How will they get the personal fulfillment that comes from being gainfully employed?

Unemployment, career upheaval, and sometimes retirement can be very difficult, but it can also be a chance to reevaluate your career path—to reinvent yourself. Every time a major shift happens in life, we have to take control of who we will become; otherwise we run the risk of never reaching our true potential.

It is said that when Albert Einstein was teaching at Princeton University, a teaching assistant asked him about a test that he'd given an advanced physics class. "Dr. Einstein," the assistant began, "wasn't this the same exam that you gave this same class last year?"

"Yes it was," Einstein said.

The assistant was confused: "How could you give the same exam to the same class two years in a row?"

Einstein replied: "The answers have changed." With the new breakthroughs and discoveries that were coming out every day, the answers that were true the previous year would not necessarily have been true even one year later. Similarly, it's said that by the time a student graduates from medical school, everything he learned in his first year is obsolete.

Likewise, the answers to questions in our own lives are changing more rapidly than ever before. If someone were to ask you what your biggest problem was a year ago, you likely wouldn't know the answer. Nor would the solution you used then necessarily work if you had a similar problem now.

Because of our fast-paced society, almost everyone is in a state of transition in one or more areas of life most of the time. This rapid rate of change is inevitable, unavoidable, and unstoppable. So knowing how to deal with change effectively is a primary requirement for living successfully these days.

We need to be flexible and allow ourselves to constantly evolve and change. We can't let our environment, circumstances, and experiences cut us off from our true selves or extinguish that inner spark. If we do, stagnation will set in and cause us to lose our *joie de vivre*. Effective leaders know that the only thing that is constant, is change. So leadership is about Planning and Hoping, that is planning for the worst and hoping for the best.

One characteristic of the most successful and happy people is that they are intensely future oriented. They refuse to dwell on what has happened in the past and things in the present that cannot be changed. Instead they focus on the factors under their control. They think about the actions they can take to create the kind of future they desire.

Throughout your life, financial changes can require you to change your life course in major and minor ways. Sometimes a major financial loss will require you to reevaluate almost every other part of your life.

In fact, many people who have accomplished great things attribute their success to losing a job unexpectedly. Rather than feeling denial, blame, or anger toward their former boss or company, they saw their new freedom as a challenge and as an opportunity to reinvent themselves and do something completely different.

Reinvention can also happen when we look around and suddenly realize, "This is not working for me," or "I'm just not happy." Ask yourself, "What do I want to create for myself? Who do I want to be?" The answers may surprise you. Use them to begin carving out a new life for yourself. Do I enjoy giving back to my community? Be coming a volunteer is a great way to give back. Do I enjoy working with kids? Tutoring is another way to achieve that. Do I enjoy mentoring managers or leaders? Become a mentor or coach. You get the idea!

If you suffer a misfortune or complication, interpret the unexpected setback as an opportunity. Change your language: instead of calling it a "problem," think of it as a "situation.". (The White House, for example, has a "Situation Room." It doesn't have a "Problem Room.") A problem is something that is upsetting and stressful, while a situation is something that you need to deal with—or even better, something you can take advantage of.

Accept what has happened as inevitable and irreversible. Refuse to waste a minute worrying about the past or something that cannot be changed. Instead, focus on the future, on the almost unlimited number of possibilities and opportunities open to you to create a wonderful life for yourself.

You can start by sitting down in a quiet place to think of all the people, places, or situations you need to leave behind. Then create a vision for the future, and imagine what it will feel like to be in that new place. Envision yourself walking away from the past and stepping into a bright and welcoming future.

Once you've glimpsed your future, you can start working toward getting there by breaking it up into manageable tasks. Make a list of your skills and expertise. If necessary, ask people close to you to help you construct it. These people can be family, friends, and coworkers. Sometimes others may be able to provide you with better insights. Give yourself an hour or two to think about this each day, and consider writing down your thoughts. Reinvention doesn't happen overnight.

Think back to the time before you got your first job. What was your dream? Not your *plans* or *goals*, but your *dream*—that farfetched idea that you spent late nights fantasizing about. If you don't have a dream or vision, it's never too late to develop one.

Where are you? Where have you been? Where do you want to be? Now is the time to dream. There are no right or wrong answers—just honest ones. If you could have any job, what would it be? What industry would it be in? Where would you live? Would you want to work for yourself, or for someone else? Do you need to make a certain amount of money? Do you need to work specific hours? Do you need to be challenged in order to keep your interest? Do you need a certain level of responsibility? Do you need to make a difference?

Compile a list of your strengths. These are the things you do well and the characteristics you possess that will always serve you regardless of your position. Are you organized and precise? Can you master complex tasks under stress? Does everyone like you? Are you persuasive, eloquent, or fearless? Consider these "transferable skills"; they will make your reinvention possible.

Find a passion, something that makes you come alive or gets the creative juices flowing. We have to deliberately choose it and not wait for it to find us, because we can easily get entangled in sadness and frustration over the past. Reinvention is thus similar to pressing the reset button; it's a complete overhaul. Make a decision that excites you. Transition from feeling desperate about where you are now; instead, anticipate what life has in store for you.

It's important that we should always be reinventing ourselves. Some experts even go so far as to advise that it should be done every five years or so. Whether or not that's feasible for you, reinvention is especially important for those who retire or lose their job, business, or money, in which case finding a new goal or purpose takes on a note of urgency.

The dictionary says that the word *invent* comes from the Latin for "to come upon" or "to find." *Reinventing* in that case would mean, literally, "finding again." It means making a completely fresh start and finding a new way of expressing something—a new way of expressing or manifesting ourselves.

As an example, Morris was a successful business executive who, when the opportunity came, took an early retirement. But even after he got out, he was always being asked questions about starting and running companies. He realized that his passion was helping others run their businesses, so he decided to open his own training and consulting firm to share his knowledge with others. He was asked to lecture and write about his business experience, and soon he was writing a book. "I never thought that teaching and writing was my passion," he says. "Many ask me if I miss the business world, and my reply is that I have the best of both worlds."

Similarly, the late Archie Davis was a man of great accomplishments: bank chairman, president of both the American Bankers Association and the US Chamber of Commerce, state legislator. But when he retired at sixty-five, he went back to school to study and pursue his passion, the history of the Civil War.

Find something that sparks your interests, and brainstorm ideas on how to tweak your skills to match those interests. Maybe you've lost the passion for hospitality that you once had. Or perhaps you no longer find meaning in your career, which has impacted your happiness. You may want to reinvent yourself as a teacher or look for work where you feel a greater connection. Regardless of your industry, you have lots of options.

As another example, George Nordhaus spent his entire working career as an information provider to the insurance industry. At age seventy-five, he launched a new venture. George is now the author of eight books and numerous articles on insurance and marketing, and he was the editor of a weekly insurance newsletter for forty years.

When you're ready to start applying for new positions, make a list of steps you need to do to get there. Do you need to meet new people? Should you spread the word? Do you need to network? Do you require training in a new field? Make it specific. Design a daily schedule so you can work toward reaching your goal one day at a time.

Chances are you'll get some negative feedback, or even downright sabotage, from your family and friends. People are resistant to change. Most of them would prefer you to stay who, what, and where you are, because they are comfortable with whom they know. You may need to be patient while others adjust to your new self and lifestyle and, sad though it may be, let go of those who aren't willing to take the journey with you. Most of all, don't let anyone talk you out of doing what you know in your heart is the right thing for you. (Refer to chapter 18 about comfort zones, and use the exercises discussed there to help your loved ones get on board with your decisions.)

Reinventing yourself can mean creating a new identity. Be gentle with yourself. You're not stuck with who you were in the past. You don't have to travel in a linear progression from who you were. There are other ways to grow. Take a leap into a new life. In fact, a jump off your current path may get you back onto a track you reluctantly detoured from many years ago.

Dare to dream of whom and what you could become, and then take steps to make it happen. It's a great adventure. It can be scary, but it can also be one of the most invigorating things you've ever done. The key is to be open to all the possibilities, including the less obvious ones. A difficult time in your current industry can be just the push you need to reinvent your career and make a positive change.

Reinvention is neither easy nor smooth. There's an old adage that says: "True courage isn't about not feeling fear; it's about feeling fear and acting anyway." Don't let your fear choose your future for you. Don't listen to negative people or the negative voices in your head. Whenever you encounter resistance, don't beat yourself up. Just ask yourself, "What can I do in this moment to keep myself moving forward?" Then do it, even if it's just a small thing.

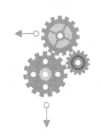

Chapter 23

The Entrepreneurial Foundation:
Mentoring the Next Generation

"Give a man a fish, you feed him for a day; teach a man to fish, you feed him for a lifetime; but teach a man to learn, you feed him for a lifetime and he doesn't have to just eat fish."
—Tim Gallwey

Tim Gallwey's saying was obviously coined for the world of business, but it is especially true when it comes to children and students—yours or someone else's. The lessons you teach them today will last a lifetime. A truly successful leader's job doesn't stop when he or she walks out the door. Mentorship is the final piece of the puzzle that will ensure that you have created a lasting legacy in whatever your career. Cultivate new managers, leaders, and entrepreneurs. And while children aren't going to be marching off to work with miniature briefcases, many of them are still open to mentorship from a very young age. But what turns a child into an entrepreneur? Lemonade stands?

Common sense tells us that it's a mixture of natural aptitude for such things (nature) and environmental exposure to it (nurture). As a mentor, the nurture part is up to you. You can inspire entrepreneurship by developing a child's emotional skills, such as

- Effective problem-solving skills
- Comfort with taking risks
- A positive attitude toward failure

Children require these skills to succeed in just about anything they do in life anyway, so the earlier you start teaching them, the better. Here are some tips to help you along the way:

o Bolster their problem-solving skills while they're young. When problems come up in a child's life, don't just dictate a solution. As teachers so famously say, "Show your work." Brainstorm solutions together. Help them identify the problem, think of all the possible solutions, weigh the pros and cons of each one, and choose the best option. The more you can break it down and talk it out, the better suited the child will be to do this on their own in the future.

o An entrepreneur's confidence when making decisions is rooted in her independence. In other words, let kids make decisions. For instance, let your child choose between having beans or carrots for dinner. Obviously, limit the choices to things that are acceptable to you. When kids are young, limit them to a few options, as they can get overwhelmed by having too many. But as they get older, loosen the reins a bit, give them more options, and trust them with bigger decisions.

o Entrepreneurs take huge risks, but being comfortable with this uncertainty doesn't happen overnight. Foster a sense of mastery in your or someone else's child—a sense of confidence and optimism. Kids need the freedom to test their boundaries and master their fears while they're young. When your child faces a risky situation, help him out at first, but transition him toward independence by making the tasks progressively more difficult and by showing your hand less and less.

o   As a parent or a friend, you can influence a child's willingness to try, fail, learn from their mistakes, and try again. This is an essential skill for entrepreneurs. Help a child learn from failure by reframing criticism into a learning opportunity. Help her brainstorm what to do differently the next time. And when you offer her suggestions for improvement, praise her before *and* after. This is called a feedback sandwich. This way, the child doesn't feel like you criticized her and takes away a positive message.

o   Kids are often taught to follow the rules blindly, but this behavior inhibits entrepreneurship. Teach your children, by example, when it's OK to question the norm—diplomatically and constructively—and when it's better to follow the rules. When it's OK to question, have them articulate their rationale. Ask, "What do you think needs to change, and why? What do you propose instead?"

It's important to note that business education starts with teaching kids how to handle money, even if it's as simple as clinking some pennies into a piggy bank to teach the child that it's good to save. But more than saving money, business is about earning money by providing valuable services to the public. The next time your child asks for a handout, challenge him to earn the money instead. Encourage your children to provide services or start a business of their own, so they can purchase the things they want now or save for bigger things later. This will teach them what it's like to own a business and manage their resources.

Another critical skill you can teach your mentee is organization. Helping them plan their schedules, staying on time, tidying their surroundings, organizing events, and the like will allow them to get the hang of being organized. A well-organized business is much more likely to succeed and remain successful.

There's a saying: "Today's kids are tomorrow's leaders." It's all about shaping a child's behavior, and you are modeling that behavior yourself. The rule is "Honesty in all things." Be truthful in your dealings with customers, competitors, and even the IRS. Don't write off personal expenses as business expenses, even if you could probably get away with it. Don't make up stories about a competitor to get more business. Don't pass off low-quality products as high-quality products. Kids have big eyes and big ears, and they will follow your example.

The business world can be cutthroat, but that may not be the lesson you want to teach to whom you mentor. If you want children or students to be respectful and honest in their business dealings, lead by example. If you follow this simple rule and encourage this ideal in your children and students as well, they'll grow up to be entrepreneurs you can be proud of.

CONTACT JACOB

Jacob M Engel, Author
The Prosperous Leader
P.O. Box 742
Tallman, NY 10982-0742 (USA)

Tel: 1.845.357.5000
Fax: 1.845.357.5007
Email:jme@theprosperousleader.com

www.theprosperousleader.com
Follow me on Twitter @JacobEngel2
Like The Prosperous Leader on Facebook